STAY OUT OF COURT
AND STAY IN BUSINESS
(Second Edition)

Clarance E. Hagglund
Britton D. Weimer
William C. Weeding
Andrew F. Whitman

©1996 Copyright Common Law Publishing, Inc.
Minneapolis, Minnesota

Copyright ©1996 Common Law Publishing, Inc.

ISBN 0-9631290-4-X

All rights reserved. Except for inclusions of brief quotations in a review, no part of this book may be reproduced or transmitted in any form or by any means, electronic or mechanical, including photocopying, recording or by any information storage and retrieval system without written permission from the publisher.

Published by Common Law Publishing, Inc.
10305 39th Avenue North
Minneapolis, MN 55441 U.S.A.

Publisher's Cataloging-in-Publication Data

Hagglund, Clarance E., J.D.
Weimer, Britton D., J.D.
Weeding, William C., J.D.
Whitman, Andrew F., Ph.D., J.D., CPCU
Stay Out Of Court And Stay In Business (2nd ed.)
  by C.E. Hagglund, J.D.; B.D. Weimer, J.D.; W.C. Weeding, J.D.;
  A.F. Whitman, Ph.D., J.D., CPCU
Includes Index.

ISBN 0-9631290-4-X $16.50 Softcover

Printed in the United States of America

CONTENTS

	Page
About the Authors	ii
Acknowledgments	iv
Introduction	v
Chapter 1 - Choosing Company's Legal Form	1
Chapter 2 - Oral and Written Contracts	10
Chapter 3 - Real Estate Purchases and Leases	25
Chapter 4 - Secured and Guaranteed Loans	35
Chapter 5 - Patents, Trademarks and Copyrights	42
Chapter 6 - Income Taxes	51
Chapter 7 - Discrimination and Sexual Harassment	60
Chapter 8 - Wrongful Discharge	69
Chapter 9 - Premises Liability	75
Chapter 10 - Products Liability	86
Chapter 11 - Business Insurance	95
Chapter 12 - Bankruptcy	102
Chapter 13 - White Collar Crime	108
Chapter 14 - Employee Health Benefits	114
Chapter 15 - Pension Plan Liability	159
Chapter 16 - Risk Management	190
Appendices	225

ABOUT THE AUTHORS

Clarance E. Hagglund, J.D. is a litigation attorney practicing primarily in insurance coverage, professional liability and other complex commercial litigation, trial and appellate. He is a Civil Trial Specialist certified by the National Board of Trial Advocacy and the Minnesota State Bar Association; a National Board of Trial Advocacy Director; a Diplomate with the American Board of Professional Liability Attorneys; a Fellow with the International Society of Barristers; and a member of the Professional Liability Section of the Federation of Insurance and Corporate Counsel. Mr. Hagglund is the senior partner of Hagglund & Weimer, P.A. in Minneapolis, Minnesota.

Britton D. Weimer, J.D. is a litigation attorney practicing primarily in insurance and commercial litigation, trial and appellate. He is licensed to practice law in Texas, Wisconsin, Minnesota, and the Eighth Circuit Court of Appeals. Mr. Weimer is the author of articles published in the <u>Federation of Insurance and Corporate Counsel Quarterly</u>, the <u>Real Estate Law Journal</u>, the <u>International Society of Barristers Quarterly</u>, the <u>Hofstra Property Law Journal</u>, and the <u>Banking Law Journal</u>.

William C. Weeding, J.D. is a commercial law and litigation attorney practicing in real estate, contracts, insurance, corporate law, partnership law, and other areas of concern to small businesses. He is admitted in both the state and federal courts of Minnesota, and practices in both the trial and appellate courts. Mr. Weeding has been a columnist for the Federal Bar News & Journal.

Andrew F. Whitman, Ph.D., J.D., CLU, CPCU has extensive experience in insurance law and risk management as Deputy Commissioner and Acting Chief Counsel for the Pennsylvania Insurance Department, as an attorney admitted to practice in Pennsylvania and Minnesota, and as a Professor of Insurance at the University of Minnesota Carlson School of Management. Dr. Whitman serves as an insurance consultant and expert witness, has authored many publications, and has taught numerous university courses and executive development seminars on risk management and insurance.

ACKNOWLEDGMENTS

A comprehensive book of this type is a large-scale undertaking. Such a project necessarily drew upon the talents and time of numerous people.

Minneapolis business consultant Susan Williams and Minnesota attorney Michelle Ulrich provided useful advice on the scope of the book and the need of all businesses to avoid the expense of litigation.

Attorney and CPA Mark Kallenbach provided the interesting and useful overview of small business accounting principles contained in Appendix 3.

The suggestions and editorial comments of Professor Samuel G. Oberstein, Ph.D., MAIR, MPH, CLU, CEBS, HIU, helped mold the complex material of Chapter 14 into an authoritative and understandable treatment of employment-based health benefits, liability and cost containment.

Secretaries Kim Smiley and Carol Soderberg provided useful feedback and patiently endured our numerous revisions. Judy Weimer and Dorothy Timm helped prepare the book's marketing. Without their work, this text could not have been produced.

INTRODUCTION

Litigation is a major threat to the financial health of businesses large and small. Suits are limited only by the ingenuity of lawyers, who daily file complaints against businesses, from sole proprietorships to major corporations. Stay Out Of Court And Stay In Business has been written by lawyers for nonlawyers -- for the entrepreneur, owner, manager and CEO who can use the information to prevent suits against them and exercise damage control if they become involved in such a controversy.

The book is user friendly, and each chapter identifies and describes in plain language the general legal principles and trends concerning businesses in general, and small businesses in particular. This book focuses on the majority rules -- the rules that are followed in most states. The claims-prevention tips identify methods that will help the reader avoid violating the legal rules. The tips will also help a business establish procedures that extend beyond the legal minimum. These tips will provide a margin of safety that will help compensate for the uncertainty of judges and juries. Finally, the insurance coverages are identified which help shield the business from the costs of litigation.

A common theme runs throughout the practical tips in the book -- the need for documentation. Successful risk management of business exposures requires systematic communication and documentation of transactions. Fortunately for the owner and manager, the same communication and documentation used in transactions can make the customer an active participant in the decision-making process. The customer who joins in the decision through discussion and documentation is less likely to be adverse in the future.

Confirming agreements in writing with vendors, employees, partners or other participants goes a long way to clarifying a verbal agreement that could have more than one interpretation. If a lawsuit does develop, that documentation can be an essential tool for the defense.

<u>Stay Out Of Court And Stay In Business</u> is not a substitute for your own judgment or experience or the advice of your attorney. If you have specific questions, or if you are involved in actual or potential litigation, we would recommend referring the matter to your attorney. Your lawyer will know if your state follows an unusual rule of law created by the courts or the legislature. If you find that a particular section of this book appears to be relevant, show it to your attorney -- he or she may find the principles and case citations helpful.

CHAPTER 1

CHOOSING COMPANY'S LEGAL FORM

John Wilson and Ann Brown were engineers at a large electronics corporation. Their jobs were eliminated when the company "downsized." They met for lunch to discuss the option of starting their own business producing fasteners for the electronics industry. However, John and Ann realized they were intimidated by the seemingly complex legal procedures needed to "start" a separate business, by the amount of paperwork apparently required to "maintain" a business, and by confusing tax options. Such fear is common but unnecessary. For the most part, the choices are not complex. Like any business decision, the person needs only to understand the pros and cons of each option and make a decision that fits the particular business.

When selecting the company's legal framework, the entrepreneur has seven options: (1) sole proprietorship, (2) general partnership, (3) limited partnership, (4) C corporation, (5) S corporation, (6) limited liability company, and (7) joint venture. Which form is best depends on the type of business and the needs of the owner(s). This chapter will examine each category.

1.1: Sole Proprietorship

A sole proprietorship is the simplest business structure. It is owned and managed by one person, who receives all of the profits and is responsible for all of the liabilities and losses. The proprietorship has no legal existence apart from the owner.

Few legal formalities are needed for the creation of a sole proprietorship. Likewise, few formalities are required for its operation. However, many states and municipalities require the owner to apply for a certificate of assumed name if the business's name differs from the owner's name. Additionally the owner must obtain a tax identification number, and may need to acquire a license to operate certain types of businesses.

1.2: General Partnership

A partnership is a business association of two or more owners, known as the "partners." The partners divide the profits and losses in the manner set forth in the partnership agreement.

The partnership agreement is normally in written form, but it can also be created by the owners' verbal agreement or by their conduct.[1] The principal characteristic of a partnership created by verbal agreement or conduct is an agreement to share profits and losses.

All partners normally share equally the right and responsibility to make management decisions, and can bind the partnership by their agreements and representations.[2] Each partner is liable to people dealing with the partnership for 100% of the partnership's debts and other legal liabilities.[3] Each partner has an ownership interest in partnership property, and has the right to use the property for partnership purposes.[4]

1.3: Limited Partnership

A limited partnership consists of one or more general partners and one or more limited partners.

The limited partnership is managed entirely by the general partners. The general partners are responsible for all of the limited partnership's debts and obligations.

The limited partners' liability is limited to their investment. In exchange for limited liability, the limited partners give up the right to participate in the day-to-day management and control of the business.

To create a limited partnership, a certificate must normally be filed with the state. Thereafter, the limited partnership must comply with various statutory requirements, including security laws.

1.4: Corporations

A corporation is an artificial "person" legally distinct from its owners. The corporation's owners are its shareholders. The shareholders elect the board of directors, and must approve fundamental corporate decisions such as sale of the business or dissolution.

Corporations will often issue written stock certificates to their shareholders. However, for most legal purposes, possession of the certificates is not required.[5]

Like limited partners, the shareholders' liability is generally limited to their investment.[6] However, if the court determines that the corporate form is a sham and that the corporation is really the alter ego of one or more dominant shareholders, the court may "pierce the corporate veil" and hold the shareholders personally liable for the company's debts and liabilities.[7]

The board of directors is responsible for the long-term management and control of the corporation. The directors are elected by the shareholders. The board of directors selects the corporate officers, who manage the corporation's day-to-day operations.

A corporation is created by the filing of articles of incorporation with the state, which must comply with the state's statutory requirements. The incorporators must select a corporate name which is sufficiently distinct from the state's existing corporations to avoid confusion. A corporation which does business in more than one state will have to register to do business in those other states as a "foreign" corporation.

1.5: C and S Corporations

A corporation may be taxed under Subchapter C of the Internal Revenue Code ("C corporation") or Subchapter S ("S corporation").

C Corporation profits are taxed twice. Profits are taxed at corporate rates and are taxed before any dividends are paid to the shareholders. When dividends from profits are paid, shareholders must also report them as income.

In contrast, the income and losses of an S corporation are not taxable to the corporation. Instead, they are passed through and taxed solely to the shareholders.

The nine requirements for an S corporation are discussed in Chapter 6, Section 3. Other than these requirements, an S corporation is organized and operated in the same manner as a C corporation.

1.6: Limited Liability Company

The limited liability company ("LLC") is a new type of business organization. It combines the limited liability of a corporation with the tax advantages of a partnership.

As of January 1995, 47 states and the District of Columbia had passed statutes authorizing the creation of LLCs. Only Hawaii, Massachusetts and Vermont had not passed such statutes.

An LLC can be managed either by its members (like a partnership) or by designated managers (like a corporation). Like a partnership, ownership is determined by "interests" rather than fixed shares of stock. Like a partnership, a person's ownership interests cannot be sold to a third party.

In most states, ownership is not limited to individuals. Corporations, trusts, partnerships, and pension plans can all be LLC members.

LLC income, gains, losses, deductions and credits are distributed to members like a partnership, based on the entity's agreement -- the member control agreement or the operating agreement.

LLCs cannot be perpetual. Most states limit the duration of LLCs to 30 years. Others require the articles of organization to establish a period of duration.

Most states require an LLC to register periodically with the secretary of state. Normally the period is two years. Failure to do so may result in termination of the LLC.

1.7: Joint Ventures

A joint venture is essentially a short-term general partnership. Rather than being an on-going business, it is formed to accomplish a limited goal.

Like a partnership, a joint venture is made up of two or more parties -- either individuals or businesses. Joint ventures enable the parties to combine expertise and resources on a joint project, without permanent entanglement.

A joint venture is created by the agreement of the parties. Frequently, the agreement is in writing. However, like other contracts, the joint venture agreement can be created by the words or conduct of the parties.[8]

Joint ventures normally have four components: (1) joint right of control, (2) joint ownership interest, (3) joint right to share in profits, and (4) joint responsibility for losses.[9] Collaborative business enterprises with these characteristics will be joint ventures, even if they are referred to by the parties as a "partnership" or by some other label.[10]

Like partners, participants in a joint venture have unlimited personal liability for the venture's debts and obligations. Like partnerships, the joint venture itself is not a taxable entity.[11] The venture's income, losses, credits and deductions pass through to the co-venturers. Allocation of these attributes is governed by the joint venture agreement.

1.8: Practical Tips

1. To reduce personal exposure for business debts and liabilities, avoid partnerships and joint ventures.

2. To eliminate double taxation of profits, avoid the C corporation.

3. For a new business, consult with your lawyer about the pros and cons of the S corporation and the limited liability company frameworks for your company.

4. For an existing C corporation, partnership or joint venture, consult with your lawyer about the pros and cons of switching to an S corporation or LLC framework.

1. Welker v. Langtry Farm Partnership, 463 N.W.2d 97, 100 (Iowa Ct. App. 1990).
2. U.P.A. §§13-15.
3. U.P.A. §9.
4. U.P.A. §§18(a) and 27.
5. Renner v. Wurdeman, 434 N.W.2d 536, 540 (Neb. 1989).
6. Becherer v. Merrill Lynch, Pierce, Fennery, Smith, Inc., 43 F.3d 1054, 1064 (6th Cir. 1994).
7. National Automotive Trading Corp. v. Pioneer Trading Co., Inc., 46 F.3d 842, 843-44 (8th Cir. 1994).
8. Ethan Dairy Products v. Austin, 448 N.W.2d 226, 228 (S.D. 1989).
9. Evans v. Thompson, 140 Cal. Rptr. 525, 527 (1977).
10. Matanuska Valley Bank v. Arnold, 223 F.2d 778, 780 (9th Cir. 1955).
11. Treas. Reg. § 301.7701-3(a).

CHAPTER 2

ORAL AND WRITTEN CONTRACTS

After starting their business, John Wilson and Ann Brown soon learned their first lesson in contracts and how they govern business transactions. They ordered 10,000 clips from the Anderson Stamping Company to be delivered in 30 days. The transaction was over the phone, and John told the ordertaker at Anderson that he wanted 10,000 clips at $.10 each to be delivered in 30 days. John did not prepare a purchase order nor did Anderson confirm the sale by sales invoice.

Thirty days after the phone call, Anderson delivered 20,000 clips at $.15 a clip. This experience taught John to avoid such misunderstandings by reducing contracts to writing.

This chapter will examine the general principles of contract formation and enforcement, then consider the features of some commonly-used contracts.

2.1: General Principles

A contract is a legally enforceable agreement. It requires (1) an offer, (2) an acceptance, and (3) consideration.

Although generally in written form, a contract can often be created verbally or by the parties' conduct.[1] However, under the Statute of Frauds, four types of business contracts must be in writing: (a) contracts for the sale of goods over $500, (b) contracts for the sale of land, (c) contracts which cannot be performed within one year, and (d) contracts to pay another's debt. Such written contracts can be informal, but they must contain the essential elements of the agreement and be signed by the other party.[2]

If a written contract is unambiguous, it will be interpreted without reference to outside evidence of what the parties intended.[3] If a written contract term is ambiguous, evidence of the parties' intent on that issue will be admitted to clarify the ambiguity.[4]

No contract is formed until the parties agree on all material terms. That is, the "offer" and "acceptance" must be identical in all material respects. An "acceptance" which materially differs from the offer is treated as a counteroffer for a different contract.[5]

An offer cannot be accepted after the offer terminates. Termination can occur in several ways. First, the offer may be rejected. Second the offer may require acceptance within a certain time. Third, the party making the offer may die. Fourth, the offering party may expressly revoke the offer.

If the agreement fails to specify details of the transaction, the courts will generally fill in those gaps with principles derived from law, general business practices, and the course of dealings between the parties.[6] However, failure to agree upon major issues may render the contract unenforceable.[7]

The "consideration" requirement is easily satisfied. It simply means that something of value must be exchanged for the agreement -- the courts will not enforce gratuitous premises. A nominal amount such as $1 is usually sufficient. Additionally, the item of value need not be monetary but can consist of beneficial conduct or a premise of future conduct.[8]

2.2: Unenforceable Contracts

Five categories of contracts will not be enforced by the courts.

First, the Sherman Anti-Trust Act states that every contract in restraint of trade or commerce is illegal.[9] Nonetheless, not all contracts in restraint of trade are unenforceable. Courts will examine the purpose, market power, and anti-competitive effect of the restraint to determine if it is reasonable.[10]

Second, a contract will be found unenforceable if it constitutes an act prohibited by law. For example, a contract which involves the commission of a crime is unenforceable.[11] Similarly, an agreement to engage in discriminatory conduct is unenforceable.[12] If a contract contains legal and illegal components which can be separated, the legal components will be enforceable.[13]

Third, a contract which violates public policy is unenforceable.[14] Examples of public policy reasons for voiding a contract include unconscionability,[15] immorality, and harm to the public[16].

Fourth, performance of a useless act will not be required.[17]

Fifth, a contract which is impossible to perform will not be enforced. However, mere difficulty of performance will not render the contract unenforceable.[18]

2.3: Breach of Contract

A contract can be "breached" in two basic ways. First, a party can fail to fully perform a contractual duty.[19] Second, a party can repudiate a future contractual duty.[20]

When one party has breached the contract, the other party has three options. First, the other party can consider the contract void, refuse to perform its own obligations, and sue for restitution. Second, the other party can sue for "specific performance" -- for a court order requiring the breaching party to perform. Third, the other party can sue for damages -- for the monetary equivalent of the value lost due to the breach.

2.4: Common Contracts

Contracts frequently used by businesses include (a) agreements to purchase or sell goods, (b) service agreements, (c) confidentiality agreements, (d) noncompete agreements, (e) agreements to purchase or sell a business, (f) employment agreements, (g) insurance policies, (h) agreements to purchase or sell real estate, and (i) franchise agreements.

2.4(a): Goods

Agreements to buy and sell goods are governed in most states by the Uniform Commercial Code ("UCC"). This ensures uniformity in transactions around the country.

"Goods" are tangible property other than land and buildings. Intangible property such as investments is generally excluded.

When the seller ships the goods by carrier to the buyer, title normally transfers to the buyer when the seller places the goods in the carrier's possession. This is known as a "shipment" contract.[21] However, if the agreement is framed as a "destination" contract, title does not pass until the buyer receives the goods.[22] Thus, the type of contract used determines which party bears the risk of damage or loss during transit.

A solicitation of an order for goods sometimes appears to be an offer to enter into a contract because it contains all the terms of a proposed contract. Nonetheless, if the solicitation is subject to approval, it is the order itself and not the solicitation that constitutes an offer.[23]

2.4(b): Services

Agreements to buy or sell services are outside the scope of the UCC. Instead, service contracts are governed by the terms of the agreement and by the law of negligence. That is, the party must perform the agreed-upon services with reasonable care.

2.4(c): Confidentiality Agreements

Confidentiality agreements are contracts to restrict the dissemination of trade secrets and other proprietary information by employees and former employees. They are commonly used in high-technology and other information-based businesses.

For a confidentiality agreement to be enforceable, it must be shown that the information in question is indeed a trade secret. Moreover, the employer must show it has made reasonable efforts to maintain the secrecy of the information.[24]

2.4(d): Noncompete Agreements

Noncompete agreements are used to prevent departing employees and principals from immediately setting up a rival business. Noncompete provisions are often included in employment contracts and in contracts for the sale of a business.[25]

Noncompete contracts are generally disfavored by courts, but are enforceable if they are reasonable and protect a legitimate interest of the employer. The test for validity is whether the restraint is necessary to protect the employer's good will or business and, if so, whether the restraint is more than reasonably necessary.[26]

Protection of confidential information such as trade secrets and customer lists will normally be considered a legitimate business interest.[27] The duration of the agreement and its geographical limits must both be reasonable.[28]

2.4(e): Purchase and Sale of Business

There are two basic ways to purchase a business: (1) buying all the assets of the seller; or (2) buying all of or a controlling percentage of the shares of stock in the seller's corporation.

Depending on the size and type of business, these contracts can be very complex. They have significant ramifications for taxes and creditors, which should be discussed with your lawyer.

The large-scale purchase of business inventory and equipment normally triggers the Bulk Sales Act. Under the Act, the buyer must (1) obtain a list of seller's creditors, and (2) notify all the creditors in writing 10 days before the sale.[29] A buyer who fails to comply with the Act will be directly liable to the seller's creditors.

Corporations are normally not responsible for the debts and liabilities of corporations whose assets they purchase. However, in most states, there are four circumstances where there is such "successor liability": (1) where there is an agreement to assume the liabilities, (2) where the transaction is actually a consolidation of the two corporation, (3) where the purchasing corporation is a mere continuation of the seller, and (4) where the transaction is fraudulent as to the seller's creditors.[30]

2.4(f): Employment and Independent Contractor Agreements

An employment or independent contractor relationship is established and governed by a contract between the business and the worker. Like most contracts, these can be written, verbal, or implied by the conduct of the parties.

A worker with all or most of the following characteristics will normally be considered an independent contractor rather than an employee: (1) payment on a project rather than an hourly basis, (2) no taxes withheld by business, (3) ownership of own tools and equipment, (4) control of own hours, (5) control of means and manner of performing the work, and (6) works for more than one business.

From the perspective of the business, taxes and benefits are far simpler for independent contractors than for employees. First, the business does not withhold income taxes or social security (FICA) taxes from the worker's pay. Second, the business does not pay unemployment taxes or half the worker's FICA tax. Third, the business does not purchase unemployment insurance or worker's compensation insurance for the worker. Fourth, the business is not required to provide employee benefits such as sick days, vacation days, pensions, life insurance, or health insurance.

2.4(g): Insurance Policies

Generally speaking, insurance policies are treated by the courts like any other contract. However, the formation of an insurance contract has some peculiarities.

The terms of the insurance contract are seldom negotiated directly with the insurance company. Instead, the insurance company is represented by an insurance agent. The agent normally has authority to bind the insurer immediately to coverage. Only if the agent lacks the authority to bind a particular risk or is uncertain about the acceptability of a risk will he or she submit the application "unbound" to the insurer.

After the agent binds coverage, the policy exists in unwritten form until the insurer issues the written policy. The terms of this unwritten policy are determined by the agreement between the business and the agent, and by the terms that are customary in the industry. In most cases, when the written policy is issued it will replace the unwritten policy.

Features of specific business policies are discussed in Chapter 11. The use of insurance policies for risk management is analyzed in Chapter 16.

2.4(h): Real Estate

Real estate is not a "good" and therefore is not governed by the UCC.[31] Instead, contracts for the sale and purchase of real estate are governed by the laws of the particular state. Thus, real estate agreements should be reviewed by a lawyer familiar with your state's real estate laws.

Real estate contracts are discussed in detail in Chapter 3.

2.4(i): Franchise Agreements

A franchise is a license to market a product or service in a standardized manner. Franchises are commonly used in the restaurant and retail businesses.

The rights and obligations of the business and the franchising company are contained in the franchise agreement. The agreement normally sets the franchise for a fixed period of time, and allows the franchising company to terminate the franchise.

There are two basic types of franchises. The first is the "entire business format" franchise. This provides standardized trademarks, services, products, marketing and research, producing uniformity between franchises in all aspects of business.

The second type is the "product distribution" franchise, which is limited to a particular product or product line, marketed under the manufacturer's name and trademark.

The Federal Trade Commission has issued "Disclosure Requirements and Prohibitions Concerning Franchising and Business Opportunity Ventures." Also, many states have statutes governing franchises. Your lawyer can provide copies of these statutes and regulations.

2.5: Insurance Coverage

The standard CGL policy excludes coverage for breach of contract claims.

Contractual liability coverage can be purchased as an endorsement to the CGL policy or as a separate policy. However, such coverage does not apply to most breach of contract claims. Instead, it covers tort liability that is assumed by contract, such as an indemnity agreement or a hold-harmless agreement.[32]

2.6: Claims Prevention

1. Confirm all verbal agreements in writing. Usually a letter to the other party is sufficient, retaining a copy for your file.

2. Review all written contracts carefully before signing them. If you do not understand a term, ask the other party or your lawyer to explain it.

3. If you are considering an agreement which could fall into one of the "unenforceable" categories, ask your lawyer for an opinion in advance.

4. Work closely with your lawyer on a drafting complex agreements such as for the purchase or sale for a business. Have your lawyer explain the significance of each provision.

5. Prepare a simple letter or agreement for employees and independent contractors to sign. The document should include a

noncompete provision. It should also require prompt notice to you of illegal acts. (See Appendix 2)

1. <u>Kingsley Associates, Inc. v. Moll Plasticrafters, Inc.</u>, 65 F.3d 498, 504 (6th Cir. 1995).

2. <u>Babdo Sales v. Miller-Wohl Co.</u>, 440 F.2d 962, 965-67 (2nd Cir. 1971).

3. <u>ConAgra, Inc. v. Bartlet Partnership</u>, 540 N.W.2d 333, 337 (Neb. 1995).

4. <u>Lone Oak Farm Corp. v. Riverside Fertilizer Co.</u>, 428 N.W.2d 175, 179 (Neb. 1988).

5. <u>Cooke v. Blood Systems, Inc.</u>, 320 N.W.2d 124, 128 (N.D. 1982).

6. <u>Matter of Estate of Hill</u>, 492 N.W.2d 288, 293-94 (N.D. 1992).

7. <u>Hsu v. Vet-A-Mix, Inc.</u>, 479 N.W.2d 336, 338 (Iowa Ct. App. 1991).

8. <u>Omaha Nat. Bank v. Goddard Realty, Inc.</u>, 316 N.W.2d 306, 310 (Neb. 1982).

9. 15 U.S.C. §1.

10. <u>Quality Mercury, Inc. v. Ford Motor Co.</u>, 542 F.2d 466, 469-72 (8th Cir. 1976).

11. <u>Seattle Times Co. v. Tielsch</u>, 495 P.2d 1366, 1370 (Wash. 1972).

12. <u>Luttig v. Bresher</u>, 383 N.W.2d 224, 226 (Mich. Ct. App. 1985).

13. <u>Keene v. Harling</u>, 61 Cal.2d 318, 320-21 (1964).

14. Restatement (Second) of Contracts §178.

15. <u>Home Federal Savings & Loan Ass'n. v. Campney</u>, 357 N.W.2d 613, 618 (Iowa 1984).

16. Johnson v. Peterbilt of Fargo, Inc., 438 N.W.2d 162, 163 (N.D. 1989).

17. Drain v. Board of Education of Frontier County, 508 N.W.2d 255, 259 (Neb. 1993).

18. Mohrlang v. Draper, 365 N.W.2d 443, 447 (Neb. 1985).

19. Metropolitan Transfer Station, Inc. v. Design Structures, Inc., 328 N.W.2d 532, 537 (Iowa Ct. App. 1982).

20. Chadd v. Midwest Franchise Corp., 412 N.W.2d 453, 458 (Neb. 1987).

21. UCC 2-509(1)(a).

22. UCC 2-509(1)(b).

23. Markmann v. H.A. Bruntjen Co., 81 N.W.2d 858, 863 (Minn. 1957).

24. Surgidev Corp. v. Eye Technology, Inc., 828 F.2d 452, 455 (8th Cir. 1987).

25. Curtis 1000, Inc. v. Youngblade, 878 F.Supp. 1224, 1258 (N.D. Iowa 1994).

26. Minnesota Mining & Mfg. Co. v. Kirkevold, 87 F.R.D. 324, 332 (D. Minn. 1980).

27. Modern Controls, Inc. v. Andreadalsis, 578 F.2d 1264, 1268 (8th Cir. 1978).

28. Lire Inc. v. Bob's Pizza Inn Restaurants, 541 N.W.2d 432, 434 (N.D. 1995).

29. UCC 6-102.

30. Fletcher's Cyclopedia of the Law of Private Corporations, § 7122 (1986).

31. Breitbach v. Christenson, 541 N.W.2d 840, 844 (Iowa 1995).

32. International Surplus Lines Ins. Co. v. Devonshire Coverage Corp., 155 Cal. Rptr. 870, 874-75 (1979).

CHAPTER 3

REAL ESTATE PURCHASES AND LEASES

After five years in business, John Wilson and Ann Brown decided they needed additional office and manufacturing space. Their business had grown significantly, and they had added office staff, a bookkeeper, two sales people, and an engineer. They located space that satisfied their needs, and came to terms with the landlord in a phone conversation. They agreed on rent at $20.00 a square foot for a term of five years.

A date was set for occupancy and John and Ann began their plans for the move. Several weeks before the occupancy date, Ann called the landlord inquiring about moving their equipment over a weekend. The landlord then advised Ann that he had rented the space to another business at a higher square foot rate and for a longer period. When Ann expressed her anger and surprise, the landlord pointed out that there was no written lease between them, and that an oral lease is unenforceable under state law.

As they researched the legal side of real estate leases and purchases, John and Ann realized that, for the most part, the issues and options are simple and straightforward. Much of the apparent complexity comes from the requirement that most real estate transactions be in writing, and from the arcane terminology used in such documents by real estate lawyers.

For example, what exactly is "real estate"? "Real estate" or "real property" consists of land, buildings, and fixtures to the land and buildings. Lawyers use the term "real" property to distinguish it from portable "personal" property.

This chapter will discuss the three principal means used by businesses to acquire possession of real property: purchases, contracts for deed, and leases. That is, the business can either be a present owner, a future owner, or a tenant.

3.1: Real Estate Purchases

Ordinarily, the sale of real estate takes place in two stages: a purchase agreement, followed by a closing. The purchase agreement is a contract to purchase at a future date. The closing is the actual transfer of ownership. Financing is normally by a mortgage.

3.1(a): Purchase Agreement

Purchase agreements are sometimes referred to as "contracts of sale" or "earnest money contracts." However, when applied to real estate, the meaning is the same -- a contract or agreement to transfer ownership.

The purchase agreement fixes a date for the closing -- usually between 30 to 90 days after the signing of the purchase agreement. The agreement also identifies the property, the parties, the purchase price, and any other items of importance to the parties. Some states also require the purchase agreement to contain the terms of financing.[1]

The purchase agreement will also identify conditions which must occur before the parties are obligated to close. A common condition is that the purchaser be able to obtain financing.[2]

Unless the purchase agreement says otherwise, courts will also imply in the purchase agreement a covenant that the title is "marketable".[3] This does not require a perfect title, but only one that is free from all reasonable risk of attack. For example, contamination by petroleum discharge does not necessarily preclude marketable title.[4] Ordinarily, the title need not be marketable until the date of the closing.

3.1(b): Closing

The heart of the closing is the transfer of ownership. This is done by a "deed" -- a document which conveys title to the purchaser. A deed must be in writing to be enforceable.

Like a purchase agreement, the deed must identify the parties and the land. It must be signed by the seller, and state a present intent to convey ownership. If the deed is ambiguous, testimony will be taken from the parties to clear up the ambiguity.[5]

A "warranty" deed contains various assurances about the transaction: that the seller has the right to convey title, that there are no encumbrances to the property, that the purchaser will not be disturbed in its future possession of the property, and other similar promises.

In contrast, a "quit claim" deed expressly states that it makes no warranties. The seller simply conveys whatever interest in the property it possesses.

Following the conveyance by deed, title should be promptly recorded. Unrecorded titles are still enforceable between the parties. However, recording a conveyance gives the purchaser priority over others who claim an unrecorded interest in the same property.

3.1(c): Mortgages

Most real estate purchases are financed with a "mortgage." A mortgage provides an ownership or security interest in favor of the lender, and establishes periodic payments for repayment of the loan and extinguishment of the mortgage.

There are two basic types of mortgages. The traditional mortgage involves equal payment over a substantial number of years. The "balloon" type mortgage involves short-terms of three to five years, in which the purchaser makes interest-only payments or only nominal payments of principal. The principal then becomes due or "balloons" at the end of the term. Though the demand for the full principal can produce harsh results, it will normally be enforced by the courts.[6]

The mortgage gives the lender the right to foreclose if the purchaser defaults. The most common form of default is failure to make timely mortgage payments. However, depending on the language of the contract, security agreement or mortgage, default can also be caused by the unauthorized sale or transfer of the property,[7] failure to insure,[8] or failure to pay taxes.[9] Under an "acceleration" clause, if the purchaser defaults, the lender can declare the full debt due and payable.[10]

To exercise its right to foreclose, the lender must provide notice or take some affirmative action showing its intention to accelerate. In most, states, the purchaser can then avoid foreclosure by paying the lender all past-due amounts.

If foreclosure proceeds, the lender may go through the courts. This is known as "judicial foreclosure." If the borrower defends, it will have a right to trial. If the borrower does not respond, the lender will obtain a default judgment of foreclosure. Once foreclosure is ordered, the lender obtains the right to possess and sell the property.

This judicial foreclosure process can be avoided if the mortgage contains a power-of-sale provision. After providing notice, the lender can proceed directly to public sale of the property.

If a surplus results, all other parties with security interests in the property may then be paid. Only after all secured parties are paid will any surplus be returned to the purchaser.

3.1(d): Title Insurance

Title insurance is an insurance policy that protects the lender if title defects are found after the closing. Most lenders require such insurance as a condition of the loan.

Title insurance can also be purchased protecting the real estate purchaser, an option which you may want to discuss with your attorney. These purchaser policies are included automatically in some states.

Title insurance protects against hidden defects in the chain of ownership such as forgeries, misdescriptions of property, and defects in the transfer procedure between prior owners. The policies will list and exclude defects of which the title insurance company is aware, zoning restrictions, and unfiled mechanic's liens.

Some title policies have an "accurate survey" condition.[11]

Title insurance is limited to the face value shown on the policy. It is also limited to defects which arose before the policy's effective date.

3.2: Contracts for Deed

The contract for deed is also known as the "installment land contract" or the "long-term land contract." It is used essentially as a financing device, when a conventional mortgage is unavailable or unacceptable to the parties.

Under a contract for deed, the purchaser obtains immediate possession of the property in exchange for an agreement to make monthly installment payments until the property is paid for. The payments can last for as little as two years to as much as 30 years.

During this payment period, the seller retains legal title. When the contract is paid off, the seller transfers title to the purchaser.

Most contracts for deed provide that, if the purchaser defaults, the contract is breached and the seller may retake possession of the property. The past payments are forfeited and the purchaser is relieved of all future obligations. However, the result can be harsh, especially when the purchaser is close to the end of the contract. Therefore, courts are reluctant to enforce such forfeiture provisions unless default is substantial.[12] In addition, many state statutes provide for "grace periods" during which the defaulting purchaser can bring payments up to date and avoid forfeiture.

3.3: Leases

A lease provides possession of the property in exchange for periodic lease payments. Absent a purchase option, there is no transfer of ownership.

Like most real estate agreements, a lease must identify the essential terms: the parties, the property, the payments, the duration of the lease, and any other terms important to the parties. Generally speaking, a lease must be in writing to be enforceable. However, many states allow short-term leases (such as less than one year) to be verbal. Also, in most states the exercise of an option to renew can be done verbally.[13]

A purchase option, if included, is essentially an irrevocable offer by the landlord to sell the property to the tenant.[14] Generally, the option expires at the end of the lease term. However, the lease may fix an earlier date. Additionally, leases often require the tenant to provide notice of intent to exercise the option by a deadline prior to the lease's expiration. The tenant's failure to meet such deadlines makes the purchase option unenforceable.[15]

Ordinarily, a covenant of "quiet possession" will be implied in the lease. This promises that the landlord and its representatives will not disturb the tenant's peaceable possession and enjoyment of the property. Many states require other covenants in leases, such as an agreement by the landlord to keep the premises in reasonable repair and to comply within state's health and safety laws.

The lease will normally describe acts which constitute default by the tenant, allowing the landlord to terminate the lease and reenter the property. Common acts of default are failure to pay rent, tenant insolvency, and abandonment of the premises.

Under most leases, the tenant has a duty to maintain the property in suitable condition during the lease and surrender it in suitable condition at the end of the lease. Failure to do so makes the tenant liable to the landlord for monetary damages.[16]

3.4: Practical Tips

1. When acquiring commercial property, analyze the pros and cons of a direct purchase, a contract for deed, and lease.

2. On a direct purchase or contract for deed, consider purchasing title insurance for yourself as well as for the lender.

3. If you have a mortgage, ask your attorney how much notice you are entitled to under the mortgage and under state law prior to foreclosure.

1. Trotter v. Allen, 234 So.2d 287, 289-90 (Ala. 1970).
2. See Bushmiller v. Schiller, 368 A.2d 1044 (Md. Ct. App. 1977).
3. Laba v. Carey, 327 N.Y.S.2d 613, 621 (1971).
4. Vandervort v. Higginbotham, 634 N.Y.S.2d 800, 801 (1995).
5. United States v. Zorger, 407 F.Supp. 25, 30 (E.D. Pa. 1976).
6. Barck v. Grant State Bank, 357 N.W.2d 872, 874 (Mich. Ct. App. 1984).
7. Cagan v. Intervest Midwest Real Estate Corp., 774 F.Supp. 1089, 1091 (N.D. Ill. 1991).
8. Bowen v. Danna, 637 S.W.2d 560, 564 (Ark. 1982).
9. Carpenter v. Riley, 675 P.2d 900 (Kan. 1984).
10. Ciavarelli v. Zimmerman, 593 P.2d 697, 699 (Ariz. 1979).
11. Muscat v. Lawyers Title Ins. Corp., 351 N.W.2d 893, 895-96 (Mich. Ct. App. 1984).
12. Nigh v. Hickman, 538 S.W.2d 936, 937 (Mo. Ct. App. 1976).
13. Gruber v. Castleberry, 533 P.2d 82, 83 (Ariz. Ct. App. 1975).
14. In re Marriage of Joaquin, 239 Cal. Rptr. 175, 176 (1987).
15. Catawba Athletics Inc. v. Newton Car Wash Inc., 281 S.E.2d 676, 679-80 (N.C. Ct. App. 1981).
16. Northwest Commerce v. Continental Data Forms, Inc., 598 N.E.2d 446, 448 (Ill. Ct. App. 1992).

CHAPTER 4

SECURED AND GUARANTEED LOANS

For the initial start-up costs of Wilson & Brown Engineering, John Wilson and Ann Brown had to scramble for funds. After using up their personal savings and charging the limits on their charge cards, they considered commercial loans.

The loan policy of Wilson & Brown's bank required collateral, a personal guaranty, or both. This added risk showed John and Ann the high cost of borrowed money.

Banks, vendors and other lenders seldom will loan money to a business without some sort of security interest and/or personal guaranty in case of default. Absent such "backup", the lender has little chance of recovery in case of default.

4.1: Simple Loans

A loan with no security interest or guaranty is a high-risk proposition for the lender. If the business defaults, the lender's only recourse is an expensive lawsuit against what is probably an almost-insolvent business. By the time the lender has prevailed in court and obtained a collectible judgment, it is likely the business will either be bankrupt or lack any substantial assets.

Because of this risk of default, lenders will seldom offer loans without a personal guaranty or a security interest. When such unsecured and unguaranteed loans are available, they normally have high interest rates to compensate for the lender's increased risk.

4.2: Personal Guarantees

A personal guaranty by a business owner provides the lender with some comfort. A personal guaranty is a separate contract which enables the lender to sue the guarantor for the debt if the business defaults.

The guarantor's liabilities are generally limited to the scope of the debtor's liabilities. Thus, the satisfaction of the debt will extinguish the guarantee.[1]

For obvious reasons, most business owners seek to avoid signing personal guarantees. However, the practice of requiring a personal guaranty has become common both with lenders and with trade creditors on large purchases.

Personal guarantees are unenforceable if: (1) the guarantor received little or nothing in exchange for the guaranty, and (2) enforcement of the guaranty would render the guarantor insolvent.[2]

4.3: Security Interests

A security interest gives the lender the right to immediate or at least expedited possession of specified property if the business defaults on the loan.

4.3(a): Creation of Security Interest

The creation of an enforceable security interest is a two-step procedure. First, the business must sign a security agreement.[3] The security agreement will identify the parties, the loan, the collateral, and the conditions for default.

Second, the security interest must be "perfected." This takes place when the lender either files a financing statement or takes possession of the collateral.[4] With equipment, inventory and other collateral needed by the business to operate, the lender will normally perfect the security interest by filing. With "paper" collateral such as title documents, the lender will normally perfect the security interest by possession of the paper.

For a financing statement to be effective, it must be accurate. Thus, use of the debtor's trade name rather than its legal name may void the filing.[5]

4.3(b): Default and Collateral

In case of default, the lender need not wait for a judgment to obtain possession and ownership of the collateral. First, the law normally allows the lender to engage in "self help" by simply taking possession of the collateral and selling it to satisfy the debt.

However, the lender may not take possession of the collateral if it would result in a breach of the peace.[6] A "breach of the peace" is an unauthorized entry into the debtor's home or building, or entry onto the debtor's land if the debtor objects.[7]

Additionally, the lender cannot sell the property using a commercially unreasonable procedure.[8]

Finally, before selling the property, the lender must notify the business of the sale date and give the business an opportunity to redeem the collateral by paying the full amount of the debt.[9]

Second, if self-help repossession fails, the lender can bring suit and obtain an immediate court order requiring the business to turn over the collateral and authorizing the lender to sell it.

If sale of the collateral does not completely satisfy the debt, the lender can normally seek a deficiency judgment for the remainder. Like a lawsuit to collect an unsecured debt, an action for a deficiency judgment is often more expensive to the lender than the likely recovery.

4.4: Garnishment

In a garnishment proceeding, the court orders a third party holding the income, funds or other assets of a debtor to turn them over to the creditor. This is significant for a business in two ways:

(a) when the business is the debtor, and (b) when an employee is the debtor.

4.4(a): Business as Debtor

If the business is the debtor, funds owed the business will be subject to garnishment. The most common target is the business' bank accounts. Additionally, if the creditor follows the correct procedures, it can also obtain rights to the proceeds of promissory notes and other negotiable instruments payable to the business.[10]

However, most of the business' unliquidated claims are not subject to garnishment. For example, a conditional contract is not subject to garnishment until the condition is satisfied.[11] Likewise, a verdict won by the business is not ordinarily subject to garnishment until collected upon.[12]

4.4(b): Employee as Debtor

If the employee is the debtor, the business may be required to cooperate with a court order garnishing the employee's wages and benefits. Once the garnishment order is issued, the business must comply. If the business wishes to help the employee avoid wage garnishment, it must help the employee defend against the garnishment complaint prior to the issuance of the order.

A creditor is not entitled to garnish all of the employee's income, even for an undisputed debt. Federal law generally limits garnishment to 25% of the employee's wages.[13] A higher percentage may be garnished for alimony or child support -- between

50% and 65%, depending on the dependency status of the person receiving the support and the delinquency of the payments.[14] All states have some income exemptions, some of which are stricter than federal law.

4.5: Practical Tips

1. To reduce personal exposure for business debts, the owners should, whenever possible, avoid giving personal guarantees.

2. If you are experiencing financial difficulties, be aware of which debts owed the business are liquidated and which are unliquidated.

3. Keep track of which business assets are collateral for debt, and ask your attorney what methods your states allows for protecting those assets from "self-help" repossession by creditors.

1. Restatement Security §122.
2. 11 U.S.C. § 548(a)(2)(B).
3. UCC 9-204(1).
4. UCC 9-302.
5. UCC 9-402, Comment 7.
6. UCC 9-503.
7. Girard v. Anderson, 257 N.W. 400, 401 (Iowa 1934).
8. UCC 9-504(1).
9. UCC 9-506.
10. West v. Baker, 510 P.2d 731, 733 (Ariz. 1973).
11. Walker v. Paramount Engineering Co., 353 F.2d 445, 450 (6th Cir. 1965).
12. McIlroy Bank v. First Nat. Bank, 480 S.W.2d 127, 128 (Ark. 1972).
13. 15 U.S.C. § 1673(a).
14. 15 U.S.C. § 1673(b).

CHAPTER 5

PATENTS, TRADEMARKS AND COPYRIGHTS

As Wilson & Brown developed their own products and processes, they became concerned about these secrets being copied by competitors. John and Ann had a general notion that there should be legal protection for these confidential ideas, but decided they should educate themselves about the specifics.

Legal protection for patents, trademarks and copyrights can help secure the business' ownership rights in its ideas. These are often referred to collectively as "intellectual property."

5.1: Patents

A patent is a government document that both fully discloses an invention and establishes the rights of the inventor. Through a patent, the government grants the inventor, for a limited time, the right to exclude others from making, using or selling the invention. In exchange, the inventor gives up the right to keep the invention secret.

Patentable inventions include process, machines, articles of manufacture, composition of matter, biotechnology, computer software, ornamental designs, and improvements on any of the above.[1]

Nonpatentable inventions include ideas, inventions depending entirely on printed matter, methods of doing business, and naturally-occurring products.

For a patent to be awarded, the invention must have three characteristics. First, it must be useful.[2] Second, it must be "novel" -- that is, it must not have been publicly disclosed or used prior to the patent application.[3] Third, it must be "unobvious" -- that is, not a simple combination of pre-existing patents.[4]

Most patents last 17 years from the date of issuance.[5] However, there is a 14-year period for "design" patents -- for ornamental designs of useful objects.[6] Additionally, pharmaceutical patents may be extended to make up for time lost due to government-mandated testing.[7] Finally, a special act of Congress can extend a patent.[8]

Patent applications are filed with the U.S. Patent and Trademark Office. The application will normally require a detailed description of the invention, one or more claims that define the scope of the invention, and drawings of the invention.

The patent application must be submitted by the inventor. However, after the patent is issued, it can be sold to another party.[9]

In addition, the patent holder can license another person or business to use the invention.

An employee hired to invent may be required to assign the patent to the employer, especially if the employee uses the employer's equipment and facilities to make the invention. However, to eliminate any uncertainty on this issue, the business should include a sentence in the employment contract requiring assignment of patents.

To help prove inventorship, the business should do three things. First, the business should mail a written description of the invention to itself. Second, the business should prepare a detailed written description and drawing of the invention, signed and dated by the inventor. Third, the invention should be verbally explained to a trustworthy witness, who will sign and date a statement that they have read and understood the description and will keep the invention confidential.

A patent is "infringed" by the unauthorized making, using or selling of the patented invention.[10] In response, the holder of the patent may go to court and seek monetary damages and an injunction.[11] An "injunction" is a court order prohibiting the other person from continuing with the infringement.

5.2: Trademarks

A "trademark" is a word, name, symbol, or device which (1) identifies a person's goods, (2) distinguishes the goods from those manufactured by others, and (3) indicates the source of the goods.[12]

To be registered, a trademark must be distinctive.[13] Generic words cannot be used. Neither can marks which are so similar to an existing trademark as to cause mistake or confusion between the two.

In addition, the mark cannot be (1) merely descriptive of the goods; (2) geographically descriptive; (3) merely a surname; (4) the name, portrait or signature of a living person, unless consent is given; (5) immoral, deceptive or scandalous.[14]

The user of a trademark in interstate commerce acquires legal right to its use without federal registration. However, as a practical matter, federal registration firmly establishes ownership to the public and decreases the chances of infringement. An application to register a trademark is filed with the U.S. Patent & Trademark Office.

Federal registration requires "use in commerce" -- actual usage in the ordinary course of trade.[15] Application can be made prior to use in commerce, with registration contingent on its future use.[16]

A trademark is "infringed" by a use of a mark so similar that it is "likely" to cause confusion or mistake.[17] Actual confusion or mistake need not be proven.

Under the "fair use" exception, similar mark can be used if there is no likelihood of confusion.[18]

Like patent infringement, a suit can be brought for trademark infringement seeking damages and an injunction.

Unlike copyrights or patents, there is no fixed time period for trademarks. They can last indefinitely as long as the owner continues to use the mark to identify its goods or services. However, federal trademark registration must be renewed every ten years.

5.3: Copyright

A copyright protects original works of authorship.[19] Examples include literary works, musical works, dramatic works, choreographic works, graphic and sculptural works, motion pictures and other audio-visual works, sound recordings, and architectural works.[20]

Generally speaking, the copyright owner has the exclusive right to reproduce, adapt, publish, publicly perform and publicly display the work for a fixed period of time.[21] However, under the "fair use" exception, the work can be reproduced for purposes of criticism, comment, news reporting, scholarship and research.[22]

A copyright protects the way ideas are compiled and expressed, but does not protect the underlying ideas, facts, procedures, processes and concepts.[23] If a person adds to a pre-existing work, a copyright covers only the elements added.[24]

A copyright automatically vests in the author(s).[25] In a joint work, the joint authors both have copyright interests, despite any differences in their contributions.[26] However, a collaborator who merely provides ideas and concepts for a copyrighted work is not a co-author.[27] Absent a contrary written agreement, work created by an employee for the employer is considered the work of the employer.[28] Like a patent, a copyright can be sold or licensed to another.[29]

The copyright begins with the creation of the work and ends 50 years after the author's death.[30] Copyrights on "works for hire" made by employees last 75 years from the date of publication or 100 years from the date of creation, whichever is less. A copyright may be registered any time before it expires. A person applies for copyright protection on forms provided by U.S. Copyright Office.

Registration is not a condition of copyright protection.[31] The copyright is automatic at the time the author's work is fixed in a tangible form and can be understood. The intent to copyright can be shown by placing the copyright symbol on the WWL with the date and author's name. For example: ©1995 Jane Doe. However, copyright registration is a prerequisite to a federal infringement suit.[32] Like trademarks and patents, a copyright infringement action can seek both an injunction and damages.[33]

Copyright registration information can be obtained from the Register of Copyrights, Library of Congress, Washington, D.C. 20559.

5.4: Insurance Coverage

The standard CGL policy provides coverage for claims that the business advertising infringed on a competitor's copyright.

5.5: Practical Tips

1. Keep records to document when and how your company's works and inventions were developed.

2. Use a signed, written agreement to assign or receive the assignment of any copyright, patent or trademark.

3. Use a signed, written agreement clarifying ownership with any employee or independent contractor involved in the production of a product or work.

4. Promptly register all copyrights, patents and trademarks.

1. 35 U.S.C. §§101, 161, 171.
2. 35 U.S.C. §101.
3. 35 U.S.C. §102.
4. 35 U.S.C. §103.
5. 35 U.S.C. §154.
6. 35 U.S.C. §173.
7. 35 U.S.C. §§155-56.
8. <u>Id.</u>
9. 35 U.S.C. §261.
10. 35 U.S.C. §§271(a), 163, 171.
11. 35 U.S.C. §283-284.
12. 15 U.S.C. §1127.
13. 15 U.S.C. §1052(d).
14. 15 U.S.C. §1052.
15. 15 U.S.C. §1127.
16. 15 U.S.C. §1051(b).
17. 15 U.S.C. §1114(1).
18. <u>Mil-Mar Shoe Co., Inc. v. Shonac Corp.</u>, 906 F. Supp. 476, 483 (E.D. Wis. 1995).
19. 17 U.S.C. §§102(a), 301.
20. 17 U.S.C. §101.
21. 17 U.S.C. §106.

22. 17 U.S.C. §107.

23. 17 U.S.C. §102(b), 103.

24. 17 U.S.C. §§101, 103.

25. 17 U.S.C. §§101, 201(a).

26. Erickson v. Trinity Theaters, Inc., 13 F.3d 1061, 1068 (7th Cir. 1994).

27. Balkin v. Wilson, 863 F.Supp. 523, 526 (W.D. Mich. 1994).

28. 17 U.S.C. §101, 201(b).

29. 17 U.S.C. §§201(d), 204.

30. 17 U.S.C. §302(a).

31. 17 U.S.C. §408.

32. 17 U.S.C. §411.

33. 17 U.S.C. §§502-05.

CHAPTER 6

INCOME TAXES

Wilson & Brown searched for a method of reducing income taxes without burdening the business with unnecessary expense. They learned that, for their closely held (not public) business, electing a S Chapter or S corporation resulted in a significant tax savings.

This chapter will examine the basic principles of tax law for C corporations, S corporations, partnerships, sole proprietorships, LLCs, and retirement plans.

6.1: C Corporations

As discussed in Chapter 1, one of the major disadvantages of a C corporation is the double taxation of income: first to the corporation, then on dividends to the shareholders.

"Dividends" are corporate profits divided among the shareholders in proportion to their ownership of stock.[1] Shareholders have no right to dividends until the directors declare them. Dividends may only be paid out of net earnings or from the surplus of assets over liabilities.

Dividends are included in the shareholder's income.[2] However, the corporation's payment of a debt to the shareholder is not a dividend and not taxable as income to the shareholder. Likewise, a bona fide loan from the corporation to a shareholder is not taxed as a dividend.

Business transactions between a closely-held C corporation and a shareholder are closely scrutinized by the IRS. For example, in many cases the sale or exchange of property cannot be deducted for tax purposes.[3] Similarly, capital gains treatment may be denied for a sale or exchange of depreciable property to the corporation.[4] Also, stock owned by one family member may be treated as if owned by every family member.[5] Likewise, the IRS can reallocate income among corporations owned or controlled by the same parties.[6]

If a C corporation accumulates earnings over $150,000 rather than distributing them to shareholders, and no genuine business need can be shown for the accumulation, an "accumulated earnings" penalty tax will be imposed on the corporation.[7] This tax is in addition to the corporation's income tax and other taxes.

6.2: S Corporations

If the S corporation has complied with all the legal requirements of a "small business corporation"[8], its income will not be taxable to the corporation. Instead, like a partnership, income will only be taxed once -- to the owners, the shareholders. Income and expenses "flow through" to the shareholders, who are taxed at their individual rates in proportion to their shares of stock.

The principal tax drawbacks of an S corporation are that (1) it cannot deduct certain fringe benefits, and (2) the shareholders must pay tax on undistributed profits.

To be an eligible S corporation, the corporation must meet nine requirements. First, it cannot have more than 35 shareholders.[9]

Second, its shareholders can only be individuals, estates, or certain trusts.[10]

Third, it cannot have a nonresident alien as a shareholder.[11]

Fourth, it cannot have more than one class of stock.[12]

Fifth, it must not be an "affiliated" corporation. That is, it cannot own 80 percent or more of both the voting and nonvoting stock of another corporation.[13]

Sixth, it cannot be an "ineligible" corporation. These include certain insurance companies, financial institutions, domestic international sales corporations, corporations entitled to take possessions tax credit, and foreign corporations.[14]

Seventh, it must use a "permitted tax year." Ordinarily, this means a calendar year must be used, unless a business purpose can be established for using a fiscal year.[15]

Eighth, absent IRS consent, it cannot have terminated or revoked an S-election within the last five years.[16]

Ninth, the corporation must meet the above requirements on every day for which the election is to be effective.[17]

If the above requirements are met, there is no limitation on the kind of business an S corporation can conduct or the source of its gross receipts.

Changing from a C corporation to an S corporation is accomplished simply by filing Form 2553 with the IRS. It does not require reorganization of the corporation.

6.3: Partnerships

Although a partnership is treated as a separate entity for accounting purposes, it is not subject to income taxes. Instead, taxes are paid by the partners. This involves a two-step process.

First, the partnership's taxable income is computed in a manner similar to that of an individual, and an information tax return is filed.[18] Second, each partner is taxed separately for his or her distributive share of partnership income, gain, loss, deduction and credit, at the same rate as the partner's other income. Which items are included in each partner's distributive share is determined by the partnership agreement.[19]

A partner's basis in the partnership interest is initially determined by the partner's investment in the partnership. The partner's basis is then adjusted to reflect the partner's distributive share of partnership income, loss, and distributions.[20]

If the partnership agreement fails to allocate income, gain, loss or deductions between the partners, the partner's distributive share is determined in accordance with the partner's interest in the partnership.[21]

All tax elections such as depreciation and accounting procedures are made by the partnership and are binding on the individual partners. Like an S corporation or a sole proprietorship, a partnership cannot defer taxation by retaining profits.

A joint venture receives the same tax treatment as a partnership.

6.4: Sole Proprietorships

The income and losses of the sole proprietorship are reported on the individual tax returns of the person who operates the business, and are taxed at the individual rate.[22] The proprietor can offset personal income with losses generated by the business.[23] The proprietor cannot defer taxation by having the proprietorship retain its profits.

Each proprietorship asset is treated separately for tax purposes. Therefore, if the business is sold to another, gain and loss is calculated separately for each asset.

6.5: Limited Liability Companies

As discussed in Chapter One, if properly structured, LLCs avoid the double-taxation of C corporations. That is, the LLC itself will not pay taxes. Like a partnership or an S corporation, taxes will only be paid by the owners. To ensure this pass-through tax treatment, three things should normally be avoided.

First, the LLC should not have over 500 members.[24]

Second, the LLC should have more than one member, and the members should not be under common control. The IRS wants LLCs to have the characteristics of a partnership rather than a sole proprietorship.

Third, the LLC operating agreement should be carefully drafted. The drafting of these agreements is especially sensitive in states with "flexible" LLC statutes.

6.6: Retirement Plans

The tax code recognizes four types of employee retirement plans: (a) pension, (b) profit-sharing, (c) annuity, and (d) stocks and bonds. Normally, a trust is the mechanism for collecting and administering the funds. However, annuity plans do not require a trust, if the premiums are paid directly to the insurer. If properly structured, retirement plans offer two tax benefits: deduction of the contributions by the business, and deferment of taxes by the employee.

The taxation of employee retirement plans is governed by the Employee Retirement Income Security Act of 1974 ("ERISA"). Under ERISA, a retirement plan must meet certain criteria to offer the desired tax benefits. These criteria include reporting requirements, disclosure requirements, and contribution and benefit limits. Because of ERISA's complexity, you should consult with your attorney or accountant before establishing a retirement plan.

6.7: Tax Evasion

A business that takes a position it knows is contrary to the law has engaged in tax evasion, and may be subject to penalty, including fines and jail time. However, a business that takes a good-faith position on taxes that later is rejected is not guilty of tax evasion, and in theory should not pay a penalty.

In practice, it is difficult to predict whether the tax court will find a good-faith error or a bad-faith evasion. Thus, the safest course is to take a conservative approach on taxes. If you must take a position that is in a "gray" area, obtain a thorough analysis of the issue from your accountant or tax lawyer.

1. IRC §316(a).
2. IRC §301(c)(1).
3. IRC §267(b).
4. IRC §1239.
5. IRC §§267(c), 318.
6. IRC §482.
7. IRC §531.
8. IRC §1361.
9. IRC §1361(b)(1)(A).
10. IRC §§1361(b)(1)(B); 1361(c)(2).
11. IRC §1361(b)(1)(C).
12. IRC §1361(b)(1)(D).
13. IRC §1361(b)(2)(B), §1564(a).
14. IRC §1361(b).
15. IRC §1378.
16. IRC §1362(9).
17. IRC §1362.
18. IRC §§701 and 703(a).
19. IRC §702(b).
20. IRC §705(a).
21. IRC §704(b).
22. IRC §61.

23. IRC §162(a).
24. IRC §7704.

CHAPTER 7

DISCRIMINATION AND SEXUAL HARASSMENT

When John Wilson and Ann Brown started their business, they hired Marjorie Smith as their receptionist. After working at Wilson & Brown for three years, Marjorie's relationship with the company became adversarial, and she was terminated. Before being fired, Marjorie had not complained to Wilson & Brown about sexual harassment or discrimination, although there had been disagreements over the quality of Marjorie's work. Six months after the termination, Marjorie commenced a lawsuit against Wilson & Brown, claiming that one of the engineers had sexually harassed her.

Federal and state discrimination laws severely restrict the employer's right to make hiring, promotion and other employment decisions based on the applicant's or employee's membership in certain protected groups. In addition, they prohibit the creation of a work environment hostile to the protected groups.

7.1: Protected Groups

For medium-sized and larger businesses, federal law restricts employment decisions based on (a) race, (b) religion, (c) gender, (d) age, or (e) disability. The restrictions on race, religion and gender apply to businesses with 15 or more employees.[1] The restrictions on age apply to businesses with 20 or more employees.[2] The restrictions on disability apply to businesses with 25 or more employees.[3]

Many states add additional categories such as sexual orientation and marital status, and set lower limits for the size of the business.

7.1(a): Race

In theory, a "color blind" approach to employment decisions will insulate the employer. In practice, patterns of employment decisions which appear to show disparate treatment of minorities may become evidence in a racial discrimination suit. Additionally, the employer may be liable for a work environment hostile to minorities.[4]

7.1(b): Religion

A person's religion and other basic beliefs unrelated to work cannot be raised in employment interviews. For an existing employee whose beliefs are known, the employer cannot use those beliefs against the employee. The employer must make reasonable accommodation of an employee's religious beliefs.[5] Finally, the employer cannot allow a work environment hostile to an employee's religion.[6]

7.1(c): Gender

Employers may not make employment decisions based on the applicant's or employee's sex. This restriction applies to both men and women.

Another form of gender discrimination is sexual harassment. This comes in two forms. First, harassment occurs when the employee is subjected to unwelcome advances, suggestive comments or physical contact of a sexual nature which creates a "hostile working environment". Second, "quid pro quo" harassment occurs when an employee's job status is affected by acceptance or rejection of sexual advances.

A single incident generally will not be sufficient to prove a claim of hostile environment. Normally, it must be shown the harassment was continuous and non-trivial, resulting in a pattern of harassment.[7] However, one physical advance can create a hostile environment.

An employer's pattern of sexually harassing employees may be admissible as "circumstantial evidence" of a discriminatory motive in a particular case.[8]

7.1(c)(1): Harassment by Supervisors

Employers are normally strictly liable for "quid pro quo" harassment by supervisory personnel, whether or not the employer knew about the harassment.[9] The employer is held strictly liable because he or she gave the supervisor the means and authority to extort sexual favors from employees.[10]

In contrast, an employee making a hostile-environment claim may have to show that the employer knew about the supervisor's actions.[11]

7.1(c)(2): Harassment by Co-Workers

An employer may be liable for harassment by a claimant's co-workers if it is shown that the employer knew or should have known of the offensive conduct and failed to take immediate and appropriate corrective action. This is true for both hostile environment and quid pro quo cases.[12]

7.1(d): Age

The Age Discrimination Employment Act[13] protects people age 40 or older. The employee's age cannot be a "determining factor" in an employment decision.[14] Early retirement programs do not violate the Act if they are voluntary.

7.1(e): Disability

The Americans With Disabilities Act ("ADA")[15] prohibits discrimination against a qualified individual because of the person's disability. Protected disabilities include physical and mental handicaps.

Some courts have extended the ADA to non-traditional "disabilities" such as alcoholism. However, there can be no ADA claim if the alcoholism prevented the employee from doing the job.[16]

An employee is only "disabled" if the employer has reason to believe the employee has a substantial impairment.[17]

The ADA only requires the employer to make "reasonable accommodation" to the person's disability. For example, an employee's work schedule might need to be modified to accommodate public transportation.[18]

Ordinarily, a franchisor is not responsible for the noncompliance of individual stores with ADA requirements. The franchisor must have sufficient control over the stores to be their "operator," a degree of control seldom presented in a franchise relationship.[19]

7.2: Permitted Practices

The fact that a person falls into a protected class only prohibits employment decisions based on that classification. It does not prohibit decisions based solely on other employment factors. However, recovery is allowed in "mixed motive" cases -- where discrimination is one of the reasons for disparate treatment.[20]

Additionally, in limited circumstances, the person's membership in a protected class is a "bona fide occupational qualification" and may be considered by the employer. An "occupational qualification" is one that affects the employee's ability to perform the job.[21] For example, religion may be considered by a religious organization.

Finally, an employer may adopt a bona fide seniority system which has a disparate impact on members of protected groups.

7.3: Insurance Coverage

The standard CGL policy does not provide coverage for intentional acts. Therefore, in most states, discrimination claims for disparate treatment are not covered.[22]

However, in many states there is coverage for "disparate impact" claims -- where discrimination is demonstrated by showing a statistical impact on a protected group.[23]

Additionally, many states allow coverage for "negligent supervision" claims -- when the business fails to discover a supervisor's discrimination or sexual harassment of subordinates.[24]

Some courts find that coverage for discrimination claims may be barred by the "employment exclusion."[25] Other courts do not apply this exclusion, reasoning that discrimination is outside the scope of employment.[26]

Several insurers have recently introduced their own versions of an Employment Practices Liability Policy, which covers many types of discrimination and sexual harassment claims. Because these are not standardized policies, ask your insurance agent to explain the particular coverages.

7.4: Claims Prevention:

1. Endeavor to run your business in a manner which is, in fact, non-discriminatory.

2. Keep careful records of each employee's job performance. Performance problems are difficult to reconstruct from memory during a lawsuit.

3. Provide each employee with periodic, specific written reviews.

4. Issue a memorandum to new employees requiring written notification of any sexual harassment or other discrimination. (See Form 1).

5. Before terminating an employee, provide specific written notice of all problems with job performance, and give the employee a fixed period of time to correct the problems.

1. 42 U.S.C. § 2000e-2.
2. 29 U.S.C. § 623.
3. 42 U.S.C. § 12112.
4. Rodgers v. Western-Southern Life Ins. Co., 12 F.3d 668, 673 (7th Cir. 1993).
5. Wilson v. U.S. West Communications, 58 F.3d 1337, 1340 (8th Cir. 1995).
6. Turner v. Barr, 806 F.Supp. 1025, 1027 (D.D.C. 1992).
7. Moylan v. Maries County, 792 F.2d 746, 750 (8th Cir. 1986).
8. Heyne v. Caruso, 69 F.3d 1475, 1479 (9th Cir. 1995).
9. Henson v. City of Dundee, 682 F.2d 897, 909 (11th Cir. 1982).
10. Id. at 910.
11. Id. at 909.
12. 29 C.F.R. §1604.11(d).
13. 29 U.S.C. §630.
14. Gehring v. Case Corp., 43 F.3d 340, 343-44 (7th Cir. 1994).
15. 42 U.S.C. §12101 et seq.
16. Despears v. Milwaukee County, 63 F.3d 635, 636 (7th Cir. 1995).
17. Wooten v. Farmland Foods, 58 F.3d 382, 385 (8th Cir. 1995).
18. Pattison v. Meijer, Inc., 897 F.Supp. 1002, 1007 (W.D. Mich. 1995).

19. Neff v. American Dairy Queen Corp., 58 F.3d 1063, 1069 (5th Cir. 1995).

20. Cram v. Lamson & Sessions Co., 49 F.3d 466 (8th Cir. 1995).

21. International Union v. Johnson Controls, Inc., 499 U.S. 187, 197-98 (1991).

22. Solo Cup v. Federal Insurance Co., 619 F.2d 1178, 1186 (7th Cir. 1980).

23. Castle & Cook, Inc. v. Great American Ins. Co., 711 P.2d 1108, 1113 (Wash. Ct. App. 1986). But see Boston Housing Authority v. Atlanta Int'l. Ins. Co., 781 F.Supp. 80, 83 (D. Mass. 1992) (no coverage if insured knew of disparate impact).

24. Seminole Point Hospital Corp. v. Aetna Cas. & Sur. Co., 675 F. Supp. 44, 47 (D.N.H. 1987).

25. Ottumwa Housing Auth. v. State Farm Fire & Cas. Co., 495 N.W.2d 723, 727 (Iowa 1993).

26. Brady v. Safety-Kleen Corp., 576 N.E.2d 722, 729 (Ohio 1991).

CHAPTER 8

WRONGFUL DISCHARGE

After their experience with discrimination claims, John Wilson and Ann Brown became very careful when they had to fire their bookkeeper. The reasons for discharging her were entirely based on performance -- she made mistakes and was unable to run the billing program on the computer. However, John and Ann braced themselves for a lawsuit claiming a man would not have been fired under the same circumstances.

As she researched the issue, though, Ann was relieved to discover that an employee may be discharged for any lawful reason without legal liability to the employer. Discharge is "wrongful" only if made (1) in violation of contract, (2) for an illegal purpose, or (3) in breach of confidentiality.

8.1: Employment Contract

Ordinarily, the employer-employee relationship is "at will". This means it can be terminated at any time by either party for any legal reason.[1]

However, the "at will" status of the employment relationship can be modified by express or implied agreement. Typically this occurs in one of three ways.

First, the employer and employee can agree, verbally or in writing, to certain limitations. For example, they can agree that employment will not be terminated before a specific date. Additionally, they can agree that termination will require advance notice or involve certain penalties.

Second, provisions in an employee handbook or other written policy statements can limit the employer's right to discharge the employee. Usually these guidelines are construed to require the employer to follow certain procedures when discharging an employee. The guidelines are seldom interpreted to completely bar discharge.[2]

For an employee handbook to contractually modify the at-will doctrine, most states require the language to be definite -- general policy statements are normally insufficient.[3] A disclaimer in the employee handbook stating that its contents are not part of the employment agreement will generally be sufficient to avoid modification of the at-will doctrine.[4]

Third, there can be an employment contract by "estoppel", based on the employee's detrimental reliance. This may occur when the employer promises certain employment terms to a prospective employee and the prospective employee quits an existing job or moves to a new location in reliance on the promised employment.

8.2: Illegal Purpose

An employee may not be discharged in a manner which violates federal or state statutes. There are eight types of statutory limitations.

First, an employee may not be discharged based on the employee's memberships in a protected group. (See Chapter 7)

Second, under the Federal Fair Labor Standards Act[5], an employee may not be discharged for complaining about minimum wages, overtime pay, or similar wage-related matters. Most states have similar statutes.

Third, under the Federal Labor Management Relations Act[6], an employee may not be discharged for union activities. Most states have similar statutes.

Fourth, an employee may not be discharged for exercising rights under OSHA.[7]

Fifth, an employee may not be discharged for asserting benefit rights under the Employee Retirement Income Security Act ("ERISA").[8]

Sixth, an employee may not be discharged for taking unpaid family or medical leave under the Federal Family and Medical Leave Act[9].

Seventh, in most states, an employee may not be discharged for seeking workers compensation benefits.

Eighth, under the "whistle blower" statutes in most states, an employee may not be discharged for reporting the employer in good faith for a suspected violation of federal or state law.[10]

8.3: Confidentiality

Even if the termination was not for an illegal purpose, the employer should exercise great care when repeating to others the reasons an employee was fired. Disclosure of facts about a discharged employee's misconduct may trigger a lawsuit by the former employee for defamation or invasion of privacy. The safest policy is not to disclose any negative information about former employees.

8.4: Insurance Coverage

Most wrongful-discharge claims involve intentional conduct, and are therefore not covered by the CGL policy.[11]

However, in some states, coverage will be found if there was no intent to harm the employee.[12]

Similarly, there can be coverage for an unintentional violation of discrimination laws. For example, an older employee may be discharged without the company knowing the discharge violated the Age Discrimination In Employment Act. In such cases, the claim may be covered.[13]

Coverage may also be barred by an "employee exclusion." However, the exclusion only applies if the employee's conduct was within the scope of employment.[14]

Wrongful Discharge

Under some circumstances, there will be CGL coverage for wrongful-discharge claims under the "personal injury" coverages.[15]

The newly-introduced Employment Practices Liability Policy, discussed in Chapter 7, covers many types of wrongful-discharge claims. Because this is a non-standardized policy, check with your insurance agent about the particular coverages.

8.5: Claims Prevention

1. Have your lawyer review any employee handbooks and policy statements before they are issued, to ensure there are no unintended employment promises.

2. Follow the claims-prevention procedures in Chapter 7 when dealing with members of a protected group.

3. Consult with your lawyer before terminating an employee who has asserted legal rights.

4. Avoid promises of employment you may be unable to fulfill, especially for a person who will be quitting another job or moving to your city or town.

5. Provide rules and guidelines in the employee manual giving notice of the types of conduct that may result in disciplinary action or discharge.

6. Keep the reasons for discharging an employee confidential.

1. <u>Adair v. United States</u>, 208 U.S. 161, 173 (1908).

2. <u>Salimi v. Farmers Ins.</u>, 684 P.2d 264, 265 (Colo. Ct. App. 1984).

3. <u>Pfister v. Bryan Memorial Hospital</u>, 874 F.Supp. 993, 997 (D. Neb. 1994).

4. <u>Lee v. Sperry Corp.</u>, 678 F. Supp. 1415, 1418 (D. Minn. 1987).

5. 29 U.S.C. §215(a)(3).

6. 29 U.S.C. §158(a).

7. 29 U.S.C. §660(c).

8. 29 U.S.C. §1140 et seq.

9. 29 U.S.C. §2601 et seq.

10. <u>Naylor v. Georgia-Pacific Corp.</u>, 875 F.Supp. 564, 578 (N.D. Iowa 1994).

11. See e.g. <u>Smithway Motor Xpress, Inc. v. Liberty Mut. Ins. Co.</u>, 484 N.W.2d 192, 195 (Iowa 1992); <u>John's Cocktail Lounge, Inc. v. North River Ins. Co.</u>, 563 A.2d 473, 476 (N.J. Super. 1989); <u>Crum & Forster Ins. Co. v. Pacific Employers Ins. Co.</u>, 907 F. Supp. 312, 314 (D.S.D. 1995).

12. <u>Interco Inc. v. Mission Ins. Co.</u>, 808 F.2d 682, 686 (8th Cir. 1987).

13. <u>Andover Newton Theological School v. Continental Ins. Co.</u>, 964 F.2d 1237, 1244 (1st Cir. 1992).

14. <u>Terra Nova Ins. v. Chillum Corp.</u>, 526 A.2d 642, 644 (Md. Ct. App. 1987).

15. <u>Continental Casualty Co. v. Canadian Universal Ins. Co.</u>, 924 F.2d 370 (1st Cir. 1991).

CHAPTER 9

PREMISES LIABILITY

John Wilson was shocked to hear that one of his customers had been robbed and stabbed in the Wilson & Brown parking lot at night. He was even more disturbed when the customer sued Wilson & Brown for the medical bills and personal injury damages. John was surprised to hear that the suit claimed that Wilson & Brown failed to provide safeguards such as a security guard, electronic surveillance or other methods of protection, and that the lighting in the parking lot was inadequate.

Fortunately, Wilson & Brown had CGL insurance. The insurance company undertook the defense, and agreed to pay the settlement or verdict up to the limits of coverage. (Their CGL policy contained no limit on defense costs. However, some policies include defense costs in the policy limits, reducing the amount of coverage by the attorneys' fees paid to the defense lawyer.)

A business can be liable for injuries and damage on or near its property caused by (1) a dangerous or defective condition, (2) crimes committed on the premises, (3) negligent hiring of a dangerous employee, (4) pollution, and (5) OSHA violations.

9.1: Dangerous or Defective Condition

The business can be liable to customers, tenants and trespassers for dangerous or defective conditions on the property.

9.1(a): Customers

A customer injured by a hidden hazard on the business premises may sue for the injuries. Examples of such hazards include: design or construction defects, failure to provide or maintain handrails, defects in steps and landings, accumulation of ice or snow, inadequate lighting, slippery conditions, debris or obstructions, fire and explosions.

The customer must prove three things to prevail. First, the customer must show that the injury occurred on property owned or controlled by the business.

Second, the customer must show that the business knew or should have known of the hazard.[1]

Third, the customer must show that the business failed to exercise reasonable care to maintain the premises so that the physical condition of the property does not expose visitors to an unreasonable risk of harm. A property owner has a continuing duty to inspect the property to discover dangerous conditions and make needed repairs or provide warnings.[2] This ongoing duty to inspect and warn cannot be delegated to others.[3]

As a defense, the business can raise the customer's failure to notice and avoid the hazard. This defense is called "assumption of risk" or "contributory negligence."

9.1(b): Tenants

A landlord will not be held strictly liable for tenant injuries caused by a defect in the building. Instead, the tenant must show that the landlord was negligent.[4]

9.1(c): Trespassers

As a general rule, landowners are not responsible for harm to trespassers, even if the landowner fails to exercise reasonable care. However, if the landowner knows it is likely that a trespasser will be on the property, and there exists a dangerous condition that the trespasser likely will not discover, the landowner has a duty to provide warning.[5]

One category of trespassers given special protection is children. "Attractive nuisance" is a legal doctrine designed to protect children who are injured by dangerous conditions while trespassing.

A child who is injured must prove five things: (1) that the business knew that children were likely to trespass on the property; (2) that the business knew about the dangerous condition; (3) that children because of their youth could not appreciate the danger; (4) that the usefulness of the dangerous condition was outweighed by the risk it posed to children; and (5) that the business failed to exercise reasonable care to eliminate the danger or protect children from it.[6]

9.2: Criminal Acts

Traditionally, a victim of a crime, such as assault or rape, which occurred on the business property could not recover from the business. However, most states now authorize recovery if the victim can prove three things.

First, the victim must show a special relationship with the business.[7]

Second, the victim must show that the business failed to take reasonable security measures to protect customers from attack. This may include absence of security personnel, procedures and equipment.

Third, the victim must show that reasonable security measures would have prevented the attack.

As a defense, the business may show that the customer was in a non-public area, such as a room with an "employees only" sign.

A business may also be liable for crimes which occur on non-owned adjacent property, such as parking lots, if the business knows its customers use the property and the business encourages its customers to use the non-owned property for its own economic gain.[8]

9.3: Negligent Hiring or Retaining of Dangerous Employee

Ordinarily, an employer has no duty to investigate an applicant's criminal record. However, if the application process discloses a history of violence, the employer may be liable for subsequent injuries caused by the employee. For example, the employer may be liable if an employee with a known history of violent crimes rapes a customer.

Negligent retention occurs when the employer learns of an employee's unfitness or dangerous habits but fails to take corrective measures such as retraining, reassignment or discharge.

9.4: Pollution

Pollution claims against business have mushroomed in recent years. Insurance companies paid more than $12 billion for asbestos and environmental claims from 1991 through 1995, and at year-end 1995[9] Most of the losses are covered under CGL policies written prior to 1986. Estimates by some insurer organizations place ultimate environmental losses in a range from $12 billion to $91 billion for abandoned, hazardous waste-sites alone, and from $30 billion to $50 billion for asbestos.[10]

As discussed below, pollution claims may be asserted for nuisance, trespass, or violation of CERCLA.

9.4(a): Nuisance

A business that pollutes the air or water may be subject to suit for public or private nuisance.

Public nuisance requires an unreasonable interference with a right common to the public.[11] An action for public nuisance can be brought by a government agency or by a private party.

Private nuisance involves an invasion of interest in the private use and enjoyment of land.

9.4(b): Trespass

Pollution of air or water may support a claim for trespass. The neighbor must show an intentional invasion of and interference with its right to exclusive possession of its land.[12]

9.4(c): CERCLA

Under the Comprehensive Environmental Response Compensation and Liability Act ("CERCLA")[13], a person or entity that incurs costs to prevent or remedy pollution may obtain reimbursements of those costs from potentially responsible parties ("PRPs"). In addition, state or federal agencies may bring suit under CERCLA to compel a cleanup or obtain reimbursement for a government-funded cleanup.

PRPs include waste site owners, haulers, and generators of waste or hazardous substances. Under joint and several liability, any

PRP can be held liable for the entire cost of cleanup, regardless of their actual percentage of fault.

PRPs also can include successor companies. Thus, selling polluted property may not eliminate the new owner's exposure under CERCLA.[14]

However, successor liability is not imposed in all cases. Generally, a business purchasing polluted property as part of another company's assets will not be liable for the prior company's pollution unless the purchase was a consolidation or merger, or the purchaser agreed to assume past liabilities.[15]

9.5: OSHA Violations

The Federal Occupational Safety and Health Act[16] ("OSHA") governs the health and safety conditions in the work place. Under OSHA, the federal government has issued numerous occupational health and safety standards with which businesses must comply. OSHA applies to virtually all businesses, regardless of size.[17]

An employer can be fined for not keeping occupational safety documents required by OSHA.[18]

OSHA is enforced against employers through government inspections, with notices, citations, fines and penalties for violation of OSHA standards. Your attorney can obtain copies for you of the OSHA standards relevant to your business.

9.6: Insurance Coverage

Most negligence-based premises-liability claims will be covered by the standard CGL policy, if the damages are for property damage or bodily injury. However, claims for emotional distress will not be covered, unless accompanied by physical symptoms.[19]

A claim that the business negligently hired a dangerous employee will normally be covered by a CGL policy.[20]

However, pollution claims are normally excluded. Courts give full effect to the pollution exclusion.

9.7: Claims Prevention

1. Inspect your property for all obvious and hidden hazards.

2. Correct as many of the hazards as you can. Place warning signs near any hazards you cannot immediately correct.

3. If you are in a high-crime area, consider hiring a security guard or security service to protect customers.

4. Put "employees only" signs on all non-public rooms and areas.

5. Take all possible steps to minimize chemical discharges by your business.

6. Obtain expert assistance on waste storage, treatment and disposal.

7. Provide employees with a written request to notify you of any health or safety problems.

1. Bunch v. Long John Silvers, Inc., 878 F. Supp. 1044, 1047 (E.D. Mich. 1995).

2. 71 A.L.R.2d 422.

3. Daly v. Bergstedt, 126 N.W.2d 242, 248-49 (Minn. 1964).

4. Peterson v. Superior Court, 899 P.2d 905 (Cal. 1995).

5. Restatement (Second) of Torts §335.

6. Restatement (Second) of Torts §339.

7. Restatement (Second) of Torts §344.

8. Holiday Inn, Inc. v. Shelburne, Nos. 88-0592, 0593, 0594, Florida Court of Appeals, 4th Dist. (July 25, 1990).

9. Insurance Services Office (ISO) Report 1996.

10. ISO's analysis is based on a new note -- Note 24 -- to the 1995 Annual Statement that insurers submit to state insurance regulators.

11. Restatement (Second) of Torts §821B.

12. Restatement (Second) of Torts §§158, 165.

13. 42 U.S.C. §9607, Section 107.

14. Charter Township of Oshtemo v. American Cyanamid Co., 876 F.Supp. 934, 937 (W.D. Mich. 1994).

15. U.S. v. Vermont American Corp., 871 F.Supp. 318, 320 (W.D. Mich. 1994).

16. 29 U.S.C. § 651, et seq.

17. 29 U.S.C. § 652(5).

18. Reich v. Yandell, 870 F.Supp. 284, 285 (D. Neb. 1994).

19. Lavanant v. General Accident Ins. Co. of Am., 595 N.E.2d 819 (N.Y. 1992).

20. Fireman's Fund Ins. Co. v. City of Turlock, 216 Cal.Rptr. 796, 804-05 (1985).

CHAPTER 10

PRODUCTS LIABILITY

John Wilson was concerned about the company's exposure for products liability claims. As a result, Wilson & Brown used great care when designing and manufacturing their own products. Therefore, he was surprised one day when Wilson & Brown was sued for a defective switch they were distributing -- manufactured by a different company.

Consumers injured by a defective product may be entitled to sue the manufacturer, the retailer, and others in the chain of distribution.

10.1: Types of Claims

The three most common products-liability claims are for design defect, failure to warn, and manufacturing flaw.

10.1(a): Design Defect

A manufacturer is required to exercise care when designing a product to avoid any foreseeable risk of harm to anyone likely to be exposed to the product. This includes the purchaser of the product, foreseeable users, and foreseeable bystanders.

A manufacturer may not avoid its duty to design safe products by relying on other persons to make design choices that affect the safety of the product.

Under strict liability, the consumer does not need to prove that the manufacturer had actual knowledge of the product's dangers.

Generally speaking, to recover for defective design, the injured party must show that a safer alternative design was available.[1]

10.1(b): Failure to Warn

The manufacturer or seller must provide adequate instructions for the safe use of the product. The manufacturer or seller must also provide adequate warnings of dangers inherent in the improper use of the product.

Generally speaking, there is no duty to warn of obvious dangers.[2] Similarly, there is no duty to warn professionals or sophisticated users of the product dangers.[3]

10.1(c): Manufacturing Flaws

The manufacturer is liable for any danger, caused by the manufacturing process, which the ordinary consumer would not expect.[4] The product may be evaluated against the manufacturer's own production standards, as manifested by the manufacturer's other, similar products.[5]

10.2: Parties Liable

Under strict liability, virtually all parties involved in the marketing process can be liable. Ordinarily this includes the manufacturer, wholesaler, distributor, retailer, manufacturer of component parts, assembler, lessor, licensor and bailor. However, the retailer's and supplier's liability is generally limited to defects it knew or should have known about.[6]

A seller of another company's product may be liable if the seller knows or has reason to know the product is dangerous.[7] A seller may be liable based upon a failure to inspect a product.[8]

Lessors of commercial products may also be liable for foreseeable product defects. Liability extends to component part manufacturers.

Ordinarily, the purchaser of the assets of a company that manufactured a defective product is not liable for the defect. However, under "successor liability," a new company will be liable if there is sufficient continuity of business or an agreement to assume liabilities.[9]

10.3: Damages

Injuries compensable include wrongful death, bodily injury, property damage, economic loss, and punitive damages. Some states do not allow claims for economic losses when the purchaser is a business.[10]

10.4: Consumer Fault Defense

In most states, a consumer's unforeseeable misuse of the product will bar recovery. There are two types of misuse: abnormal use and mishandling. Abnormal use is when the product is used for an improper purpose. Mishandling is use for a proper purpose but in an improper manner.

In addition, in most states, the consumer's knowing exposure to conditions that increase the product's danger is "contributory negligence" that bars or reduces recovery.[11] This defense is also known as "assumption of risk."[12]

Finally, in many states, recovery will be barred by a material alteration of the product after sale.[13]

10.5: Statutory Claims and Defenses

10.5(a): Warranties

The UCC allows for the creation of express warranties, implied warranties of merchantability, and implied warranties of fitness for a particular purpose.

1. <u>Express Warranties</u>. Even if a product is not defective, the manufacturer may be liable if it made an express promise about the characteristics of the product.[14]

2. <u>Implied Warranty of Merchantability</u>. Where the seller is a merchant in the type of goods sold, the law creates an implied warranty of merchantability in the sale.[15] This warranty provides that the goods must be of average quality and be fit for the ordinary purpose for which such goods are used.

3. <u>Implied Warranty of Fitness for a Particular Purpose</u>. If a seller knows the buyer intends to use the product for particular purpose, and that the buyer is relying on the seller's judgment in selecting the product, the seller may be liable.[16]

10.5(b): Statutes Increasing The Standard of Care

A violation of a statutory standard of care may be evidence of negligence. There are numerous statutes, both state and federal, which provide safety standards applicable to the manufacture, labeling, advertising, and selling of goods. Two examples are the Flammable Fabrics Act[17] and The National Traffic and Motor Vehicle Safety Act[18].

10.5(c): Useful Life Statutes

Most states have "useful life" statutes or "statutes of repose" which limit the manufacturer's liability for used products. Once a product has outlived its useful life, there is no liability. Usually these statutes bar suits a fixed time (normally 5 to 12 years) after sale to the original purchaser.

10.6: Insurance Coverage

Products-liability coverage is available under either a CGL policy or a special "products liability" policy.

Under the "sistership" exclusion, this insurance normally does not cover the cost of recalling the product.[19] However, "sistership" or product-recall coverage is available under a separate policy or endorsement.

The standard CGL policy contains a business-risk exclusion that bars coverage for claims that a product did not perform as warranted. However, claims for damage to or destruction of the product are covered.[20]

The owned-products exclusion precludes most coverage for repairing or replacing a defective product. However, there is coverage for a claim that the business' defective component damaged the larger product.[21]

A products-hazard exclusion bars most products-liability claims. However, there is coverage for failure-to-warn claims.[22]

10.8: Claims Prevention

1. Manufacturers should test new products under a wide range of conditions before finalizing the design, and should retain documents that show the safety efforts.

2. Manufacturers should establish reliable inspection procedures to guard against manufacturing defects, and should retain documents that show these inspection safe-guards.

3. Manufacturers should whenever possible include both instructions and labels with each product warning of its uses, limitations and dangers.

4. All businesses involved in the chain of product distribution should ensure they have adequate product liability insurance.

5. For highly-dangerous products, use colors and graphics on the label which dramatize the danger.

6. Manufacturers should keep abreast of industry safety advances, and incorporate them whenever feasible into the products.

7. Have your attorney review all advertisements, brochures and other sales documents to ensure they do not make promises that increase legal liability for defects.

1. Fell v. Kewanee Farm Equipment Co., 457 N.W.2d 911, 920 (Iowa 1990).

2. Glittenberg v. Doughboy Recreational Industries, 491 N.W.2d 208, 213 (Mich. 1992).

3. Landberg v. Ricoh Intern., 892 F.Supp. 938, 943 (E.D. Mich. 1995).

4. Restatement (Second) of Torts §402A Comment i.

5. Prentis v. Yale Mfg. Co., 365 N.W.2d 176, 182 (Mich. 1984).

6. Erickson v. Monarch Industries, Inc., 347 N.W.2d 99, 108 (Neb. 1984) (supplier).

7. Restatement (Second) of Torts §§401, 402A.

8. Gorath v. Rockwell, 441 N.W.2d 128, 131-32 (Minn. Ct. App. 1989).

9. Thompson v. Mobile Aerial Towers, Inc., 862 F.Supp. 175, 178 (E.D. Mich. 1994).

10. Michigan Mut. Ins. Co. v. Osram Sylvania, Inc., 897 F.Supp. 992, 994 (W.D. Mich. 1995).

11. Jones v. Owens-Corning Fiberglas Corp., 69 F.3d 712, 719 (4th Cir. 1995).

12. Novak v. Navistar Intern. Transp. Corp., 46 F.3d 844, 849 (8th Cir. 1994); Restatement (Second) of Torts §402A, comment n.

13. McLean v. Badger Equipment Co., 868 F.Supp. 258, 261 (E.D. Wis. 1994).

14. U.C.C. §2-313(1)(a).

15. U.C.C. §2-314(1).

16. U.C.C. §2-315.

17. 15 U.S.C. §1191.

18. 15 U.S.C. §1381, et seq.

19. <u>McNeilab, Inc. v. North River, Ins. Co.</u>, 645 F.Supp. 525, 541 (D.N.J. 1986), aff'd. 831 F.2d 287 (3rd Cir. 1987).

20. <u>Honeycomb Sys., Inc. v. Admiral Ins. Co.</u>, 567 F.Supp. 1400, 1407 (D. Me. 1983).

21. <u>Apache Foam Producers Division v. Continental Ins. Co.</u>, 528 N.Y.S.2d 448, 449 (1988).

22. <u>Pennsylvania National Mut. Cas. Co. v. Kaminski Lumber Co.</u>, 580 A.2d 401, 404 (Pa. Super. 1990).

CHAPTER 11

BUSINESS INSURANCE

Ann Brown handled most of the company's insurance decisions. Their insurance agent was constantly recommending new coverages and higher limits, and Ann initially found it hard to tell when the agent was "crying wolf." Ann realized that, as in most business decisions, self-education was essential to priorities. Therefore, she decided to educate herself on the coverages provided by each of the basic business policies.

Most businesses use several types of insurance: (1) worker's compensation, (2) unemployment, (3) general liability, (4) commercial fire, (5) medical, (6) group life and (7) directors and officers. These coverages are common either because required by law or because effective at minimizing risk.

11.1: Workers Compensation

Workers compensation insurance provides recovery for an employee's work-related injury or death. Workers compensation insurance represents a tradeoff, providing no-fault benefits which are more prompt and predictable than a traditional lawsuit, but with reduced recovery.

Most states require employers either to purchase workers compensation insurance or to qualify for self-insurance. If the employer fails to do either, the employee is free to pursue a traditional personal-injury lawsuit against the employer. However, if the employer complies with the insurance requirement, it is insulated from employee lawsuits for most work-related injuries.

Worker's compensation policies normally contain "employers liability" coverage, insuring against lawsuits for accidental bodily injury arising out of the employee's employment.

Workers compensation insurance does not cover independent contractors. (For the factors which distinguish employees from independent contractors, see Chapter 2, section 4(f).)

11.2: Unemployment Compensation

Federal law requires that most employers contribute to a federal unemployment insurance fund. Most states have similar requirements. The unemployment tax is a percentage of a fixed dollar amount of each employee's wages. The percentage varies depending on an employer's experience rating. Ordinarily, independent contractors are excluded.

In most states, to qualify for benefits, the employee (1) must have been terminated rather than quitting; (2) must have worked a certain length of time prior to termination; (3) must actively be seeking replacement work; and (4) must not have been terminated for misconduct.

11.3: General Liability

Most business liability insurance is provided by a standardized Commercial General Liability ("CGL") policy. The CGL policy has three sections: coverages A, B and C.

11.3(a): Coverage A

Coverage A covers lawsuits for bodily injury and property damage. "Bodily injury" does not normally include claims for emotional distress. "Property damage" includes both damage to and loss of use of tangible property, but excludes purely economic damages.

Coverage A is limited to claims of negligence -- claims for intentional conduct are excluded. Also excluded are most claims for pollution liability, claims covered under workers compensation and motor vehicle insurance, claims for property temporarily in the business' custody, claims for faulty workmanship, and many other claims which should be reviewed with your insurance agent.

11.3(b): Coverage B

Coverage B covers "advertising liability" and "personal injury" lawsuits. Both categories are defined in the policy.

"Advertising liability" is limited to advertising claims for (a) defamation and product disparagement, (b) publication that violates a person's privacy, (c) misappropriation of advertising ideas, and (d) copyright infringement.

"Personal injury" is limited to claims for (a) false arrest or imprisonment, (b) malicious prosecution, (c) wrongful entry or eviction, (d) defamation, and (e) publication of material violating a person's privacy.

11.3(c): Coverage C

Coverage C provides premises and operations medical payments without regard to the business' negligence.

11.4: Commercial Fire

A fire policy covers damage and injury caused by a fire and similar perils, unless the fire was the result of the insured's arson.

The measure of recovery can be actual cash value, replacement cost, or stated value. Actual cash value pays the depreciated value of the property at the time of the fire. Replacement cost pays the price of a new substitute at the time of the fire. Stated value is a value fixed prior to the fire by agreement of the business and insurer.

Ordinarily, the proceeds are only payable to the insured. However, if the policy contains a "standard" or "union" mortgage clause, a separate contract is created with the lender on which the lender can collect even if the insured commits arson.

If the policy includes "business income" or "business interruption" coverage, the insured will be compensated for earnings it would have received had there been no fire, less expenses avoidable because of the fire. Normally the coverage includes a restoration cut-off date which precludes claims for long-term lost income.

11.5: Medical Insurance

Medical insurance is a common fringe benefit for employees and is mandated in some states. There are both traditional policies and alternative delivery systems.

11.5(a): Traditional Policies

Basic policies pay all or part of the following medical services: (1) hospital room and board, (2) out-patient care, (3) surgical fees, (4) physician office visits for non-routine exams, (5) physician hospital visits, (6) diagnostic lab and x-ray, and (7) emergency room treatment.

"Deluxe" policies may include: (1) dental, (2) maternity, (3) mental health, (4) vision, (5) prescriptions, and (6) home health care.

11.5(b): Alternative Delivery Systems

Alternative delivery systems involve organizations which both receive the insurance premiums and provide the medical services. These come in two basic forms.

Health maintenance organizations ("HMOs") charge preset fees for coverage, regardless of the actual treatment costs. HMOs provide free or inexpensive checkups. However, they usually provide no coverage for treatment by a doctor outside the HMO.

Preferred Provider Organizations ("PPOs") provide a reduced fee for each service, rather than a fixed fee for all services. PPOs allow treatment by a non-PPO doctor for a higher fee.

11.6: Group Life Insurance

Compared to group health insurance, group term life insurance is relatively inexpensive. The major advantages of group life policies over individual policies are reduced rates and reduced screening for health problems.

A business may also purchase "key person" life insurance, which helps provide for the continuity of the business if an essential owner or manager dies.

11.7: Directors and Officers' Liability

A directors and officers' ("D&O") policy protects the corporation and its directors and officers from lawsuits against the individual directors or officers. Although a D&O policy will not cover lawsuits against the corporation, it will reimburse the corporation for any obligations the corporation has to indemnify the officer or director.

11.8: Other Policies

Other coverages may be necessary or beneficial, depending on the characteristics of the particular business. For example, the newly-introduced Employment Practice Liability Insurance can fill gaps between CGL insurance and the employers liability coverage in a worker's compensation policy, providing coverage for many discrimination, sexual harassment and wrongful-discharge claims. See the discussions in Chapters 7 and 8.

For a complete analysis of how risk management principles should be used when evaluating potential property and liability insurance coverages, see Chapter 16.

CHAPTER 12

BANKRUPTCY

Bankruptcy offers relief for a business whose debts exceed its assets. Wilson & Brown never availed themselves of the bankruptcy option. However, John and Ann were glad it was available.

12.1: Chapter 7 and Chapter 11

Two types of bankruptcy proceedings are available for businesses -- "Chapter 7" and "Chapter 11".

Chapter 7 is the more drastic form of bankruptcy, putting an end to the business. All of the business assets are liquidated. The proceeds are paid to the creditors.

Chapter 11 allows for the continuation of the business. Under a court-approved reorganization plan, the debtor retains most encumbered property, collection efforts stop, and the business pays off debts over a period of time. Often this reorganization period lasts three years or more.

12.2: Voluntary and Involuntary

Ordinarily, it is the insolvent business that initiates bankruptcy proceedings. However, under certain circumstances, creditors may force the business into involuntary bankruptcy.

If there are 12 or more creditors, involuntary bankruptcy requires a joint petition by three or more creditors with total claims of at least $5,000.[1] If there are less than 12 creditors, involuntary bankruptcy requires one or more creditors with total claim(s) of at least $5,000.[2] Whatever the number, the creditors must show that the business is not timely paying debts.[3]

Section 12.3: Automatic Stay

Upon filing of the bankruptcy petition, creditors are immediately prohibited from further collection efforts.[4] This bars creditors from starting new collection proceedings, continuing existing collection proceedings, asserting setoffs, and using self-help to repossess collateral. The stay lasts until the property is sold by the trustee or until the bankruptcy court terminates the proceedings.[5]

During the stay, the bankruptcy trustee can satisfy a security interest by turning the collateral over to the creditor. However, the trustee is not required to surrender collateral to a creditor. Instead, the trustee can pay the creditor the value of the collateral.

Under certain circumstances, a creditor may petition the bankruptcy court for a lifting of the stay as to particular debts and assets.[6] Commonly, such relief is granted if the creditor can show either that the creditor's interest in the collateral is not adequately protected or that the business has no interest in the collateral.[7] For example, the stay will often be lifted to allow a lawsuit for which the business has liability insurance coverage.

12.4: Voidable Pre-Bankruptcy Transfers

The bankruptcy trustee can void three basic categories of pre-bankruptcy transfers to creditors.

First, most transfers within 90 days of the bankruptcy petition are voidable.[8]

Second, most transfers to an "insider" within a year of the petition are voidable.[9]

Third, all fraudulent conveyances by the business within a year of the petition are voidable. Specifically, the trustee may invalidate transfers made with the intent to hinder, delay or defraud creditors.[10]

12.5: Chapter 7 Priorities

In a Chapter 7 bankruptcy, after satisfying the secured claims, there normally are insufficient assets to pay all unsecured claims. Thus, the trustee must examine the priority of the unsecured claims. The trustee will start by paying the highest priority claims, then move down the list. Often, the low-priority unsecured creditors receive little or nothing.

There are eleven levels of priority: (1) administrative expenses, (2) ordinary business expenses, (3) wage claims, (4) employee benefit plans, (5) certain claims by farmers and fishermen, (6) consumer debts, (7) tax claims, (8) late claims without notice of bankruptcy, (9) late claims with notice of bankruptcy, (10) fines and punitive damages, and (11) interest.[11]

Under the "subordination" doctrine, the trustee will not follow the priority levels for a particular claim if (1) there was an enforceable subordination agreement, (2) a seller or purchaser of equity securities seeks damages or rescission, or (3) fairness and justice dictates a different level of priority.[12]

12.6: Discharge

A "discharge" is a permanent release from debt as the result of bankruptcy. Discharge operates differently for sole proprietorships than for partnerships and corporations.

A sole proprietorship is discharged from all non-exempt claims. There are ten categories of exempt claims: (1) taxes, (2) debts for property obtained through fraud, (3) unscheduled debts, (4) liabilities as fiduciary, (5) domestic obligations, (6) liabilities for willful and malicious injury, (7) government fines, (8) educational debts, (9) DWI debts, and (10) debts denied discharge in previous bankruptcy.[13]

Those exemptions do not apply to partnerships or corporations. In Chapter 7 bankruptcies, there is generally no discharge of any kind for partnerships or corporations. In Chapter 11 bankruptcies, all partnership and corporate debts are discharged except as ordered in the reorganization plan.[14]

12.7: Practical Tips

1. If your business is in financial trouble, consult with your attorney about the pros and cons of Chapter 11 bankruptcy.

2. Avoid Chapter 7 bankruptcy unless you plan to retire or go into a new line of work.

3. If you are a potential creditor considering a loan that would receive a low priority in bankruptcy, insist on a security interest or a personal guaranty.

1. 11 U.S.C. §303(b)(1).
2. 11 U.S.C. §303(b)(2).
3. 11 U.S.C. §303(h).
4. 11 U.S.C. §362.
5. 11 U.S.C. §362(c).
6. 11 U.S.C. §361.
7. 11 U.S.C. §362(d).
8. 11 U.S.C. §547(b).
9. 11 U.S.C. §101(28).
10. 11 U.S.C. §548.
11. 11 U.S.C. § 506, 726.
12. 11 U.S.C. § 507.
13. 11 U.S.C. §523(a).
14. 11 U.S.C. §1141(d).

CHAPTER 13

WHITE-COLLAR CRIME

Naturally, a business owner or manager can engage in and be convicted of the same crimes as anyone else -- murder, rape, drug crimes, etc. This chapter has a more narrow focus -- crimes having some direct connection to the operation of a business. These are frequently referred to as "white collar" crimes.

White collar prosecutions have increased dramatically since the early 1980s. Business owners and managers can find themselves in jail for conduct which, in prior years, would have been handled between the parties in a civil lawsuit.

The principal white-collar crimes are fraud, arson, forgery, embezzlement, receiving stolen property, extortion, bribery and racketeering.

13.1: Criminal Fraud

Federal law makes it a crime to engage in mail fraud and wire fraud. Mail fraud is the use of the mails to further a scheme to defraud others. Similarly, wire fraud is the use of telephones and other wire communications to further a scheme to defraud. Whether the fraudulent scheme was successful is irrelevant.[1]

Additionally, most states make it a crime to make false claims for payment to a government entity.

13.2: Arson

Arson is the intentional destruction or damaging of a building by fire or explosives in a manner which endangers another person. The "endangerment" requirement does not mean another person must actually be injured, only that a risk of injury be present. The building can belong to the defendant or to another person.

13.3: Forgery

Forgery is the creation of a false document or the alteration of a document with the intent of defrauding others. Often, forgery involves the signing of another person's name.

13.4: Embezzlement

Embezzlement is a form of theft. It is the fraudulent appropriation of another's property, which has been entrusted to the defendant's care. The property embezzled can be either tangible property or intangible property such as funds or information.

There is no embezzlement if the defendant intended to restore the exact property taken.[2] However, an intent to restore similar property is not a defense.

13.5: Receiving Stolen Property

Most states make it a crime to receive, buy or conceal property knowing it to be stolen.

13.6: Extortion

Extortion is obtaining another's property using force or threats. The threats can take many forms: threats of force, threats of legal action, threats of a strike or boycott, threats of testimony at trial, threats of disclosing damaging information, and threats of virtually any other conduct which would harm the victim.

13.7: Bribery

Bribery is offering something of value to government officials to benefit the briber's private interest rather than the public interest.[3] Although the item of value will normally have monetary value, it need not be cash or tangible property. Information and other intangibles are sufficient.[4]

13.8: Racketeering

In federal cases, racketeering is governed by the Racketeer Influenced and Corrupt Organizations ("RICO") Act. Many states have similar statutes.

The main elements of RICO are (1) the operation of an "enterprise", (2) through a pattern of "racketeering" activity, and (3) in a manner that affects interstate or foreign commerce.

An "enterprise" is a group of people or businesses organized for a common purpose.[5]

"Racketeering" is mail fraud, wire fraud, extortion, bribery, and a host of other federal and state crimes.[6] There must be a "pattern" of such crimes -- two or more occurrences which have some relationship to each other.

13.9: Environmental Crimes

The federal government and most states have criminal penalties for businesses that discharge hazardous wastes. The Clean Water Act, the Clean Air Act, and CERCLA all provide criminal sanctions for specified intentional pollution. Generally speaking, mistakes and accidents carry no criminal sanctions under these statutes. However, ignorance of the relevant statutes and regulations is not a defense.[7]

Liability may extend to those involved in the "chain of production" of pollution -- such as those who transport or store pollutants discharged by another.[8] Most criminal pollution statutes require that the pollution place another person in imminent danger of death or substantial bodily harm.

13.10: Criminal Liability for Business Associates

In some cases, a person can be subject to criminal prosecution for the conduct of a partner, employee, or other business associate. This can occur in two ways.

First, employees may be accountable, under the doctrine of accomplice liability, for crimes committed by their peers and subordinates. Anyone who commands, encourages or assists another in criminal conduct is equally liable with the actual perpetrator.[9]

Second, a manager may be liable for failing to control the criminal conduct of a subordinate.

1. <u>U.S. v. Jackson</u>, 451 F.2d 281, 283 (5th Cir. 1971).
2. <u>U.S. Duncan</u>, 598 F.2d 839, 858 (4th Cir. 1979).
3. 18 U.S.C. §201.
4. <u>United States v. Sheker</u>, 618 F.2d 607, 609 (9th Cir. 1980).
5. 18 U.S.C. §1961.
6. 18 U.S.C. §1961.
7. <u>U.S. v. Hayes Int'l Corp.</u>, 786 F.2d 1499, 1503 (11th Cir. 1986).
8. See e.g. Minn. Stat. §609.671.
9. 18 U.S.C. §2.

CHAPTER 14

EMPLOYEE HEALTH BENEFITS

When they started Wilson & Brown Engineering, one of the greatest shocks for John and Ann was the cost of their employee benefits. 35% of employee compensation was spent on health insurance, pension plans, and similar benefits. Talking to other business people, they realized they were not alone.

Employee benefits, including health and pension plans, can account for 25% to 45% of total compensation, and CEOs consistently rank cost containment and liability risk control as top business priorities. Fifteen cents of each dollar spent in the U.S. pays for health care, and employers bear a large share since they cover over two-thirds of Americans who have health insurance. Employers with employee health plans face a myriad of complex laws and insurance agreements.

In 1994, average payroll costs of $36,000 were apportioned as follows: Payroll 60%; time not worked (vacations, etc.) 10%; medical and related benefits 11% ($3,800/yr. per employee); legally required payments 9% (including FICA taxes); retirement and savings plans 9%; miscellaneous 1%.[1]

This chapter examines several topics that will help employers both control these costs and reduce their liability: (1) overview of insurers and plans; (2) legal obligations under group health contracts; (3) coordinating workers' compensation, employer liability, and benefit plan liability insurance; (4) managed health care and liability; (5) 24-hour coverage; and (6) tips to control health plan costs and liability.

14.1: Overview of Insurers and Plans

There are five basic types of medical and income loss benefit programs:

1. Group health insurance through plans ranging from traditional insurance to managed care/HMO plans.

2. Workers' Compensation for job-connected injury, providing medical treatment with no coverage limits or co-payments, and emphasizing prompt return-to-work objectives.

3. Income loss coverage through workers' compensation, short-term disability, long-term disability, sick leave, and other employment-based programs.

4. Other insurance with medical payments coverage includes automobile insurance providing limited medical payment coverage to drivers, passengers, and other injured parties.

5. Employer's General Liability insurance package typically providing limited medical payments insurance to customers and non-employees injured on the employer's premises.

Employers purchase health benefit plans from the following types of administering organizations:

- Employers with self-funded plans
- Blue Cross/Blue Shield
- Commercial insurance companies
- Health maintenance organizations
- Preferred provider organizations
- Multiple employer organizations (including employer associations, coalations and private purchasing pools)
- State-Run Purchasing Pools (Some state laws permit small employers to purchase health coverage through a pool run by a state agency. The Minnesota Employees Insurance Program under MN Laws Chapt. 549, 1992)
- Combinations of these and other organizations

Employers may voluntarily offer health plans to their employees, since federal and state laws do not require employer-based health plans. Only Hawaii mandates certain employer-based health coverage. Employers who elect to establish a self-funded/non-insured plan of health coverage are regulated under the federal ERISA (Employer Retirement Income Security Act) law, and health insurance is subject to state law. Many large self-funded employee benefit plans are subject to ERISA and are not subject to state insurance law. Generally, fully insured plans are subject to state regulation.

The U.S. General Accounting Office estimates that roughly 114 million individuals (44% of the U.S. population) are covered by ERISA health plans. In most of these plans, the employer purchases healthcare coverage from an insurance company that is subject to state regulation. For nearly 40% of these ERISA plans, covering about 44 million people, employers choose to self-fund and retain the plan financial risk. Because these self-funded plans are not deemed to be insurance, ERISA preempts them from state regulation, and states cannot regulate premiums, mandate health benefits, restrict pre-existing condition limitations or apply other insurance regulations. Courts have played a key role in defining the extent to which ERISA preempts state attempts to regulate employer health plans.[2]

14.1(a): Application of ERISA
(Employee Retirement Income Security Act)

ERISA sets standards which employers must follow pertaining to fiduciary responsibility, plan reporting and disclosure, and pension plan funding. ERISA applies to retirement plans described in Chapter 15, <u>Pension Plan Liability</u>, and to "employee welfare benefit plans" defined as any plan, fund or program providing any of the following plans:

- Medical, surgical or hospital care or benefits.
- Benefits in the event of sickness, accident, disability, death or unemployment.
- Vacation benefits.
- Apprenticeship or other training programs.
- Day-care centers.
- Scholarship funds.
- Prepaid legal services.

- Any benefit described in Section 302(c) of the Labor Management Relations Act of 1947, such as holiday pay and severance pay.

Employers and health plan administrators subject to ERISA have more flexibility in benefit design and less potential liability than employers subject to state law. According to a recent U.S. Supreme Court decision, employers under ERISA can change plan benefits by using plan assets to increase benefits to certain participants.[3] In claimants' suits against employers, ERISA remedies are more narrowly defined than remedies available to plans subject to state law. For example, punitive or bad faith damages are available under state law, but not under ERISA. ERISA supplies a right of action to enforce the terms of employee benefit plans, including plans that provide health care benefits.[4] An action to recover benefits under 29USCS@1132(a)(1)(B) arises when a request for benefits is denied and the denial is not reversed by the plan. Employee benefit plans must give written notice of the specific reasons for denials of benefits and afford a reasonable opportunity for a full and fair review of the denial. The defendants in such suits often include the employer that sponsors the plan and, if applicable, the insurance company, health maintenance organization (HMO), preferred provider organization (PPO), or other third party who administers the plan by contract with the employer. Litigation under 29USCS@1132(a)(1)(B) may become more complex as the relationships between health care delivery systems become more complex.[5]

14.1(b): Federal Regulation

Federal laws which affect employer liability in the establishment and administration of employment benefit plans include:

1. Age Discrimination in Employment Act
2. Civil Rights Act
3. Employee Retirement Income Security Act (ERISA)
4. Americans With Disability Act (ADA)
5. Social Security Act
6. Health Maintenance Organization Act
7. Internal Revenue Code

A large body of law applies to the application of each of these federal laws.

14.1(c): State Regulation of Group Health Insurance

Some of the more significant state laws and regulations affecting group health insurance pertain to the types of groups eligible for coverage, contractual provisions, benefit limitations, and taxation. About half the states impose a minimum number--5 to 10 persons--requirement on group health insurance contracts. Some states recently require health plan insurers to offer coverage to small employee groups from 2 to 49 persons in size. Most state insurance laws list the types of groups for which insurance companies may write group insurance. While the categories of eligible groups may vary, at least four types involving employees are acceptable in virtually all states:

1. Individual employer groups

2. Negotiated trusteeships (Taft-Hartley Trust)
3. Trade associations
4. Labor union groups

Other types of groups, including multiple employer trusts (MET) (described in Sections 15.2 and 15.3 of Chapter 15), are also acceptable in some states, and some states have no laws regarding the type or size of groups.

14.1(d): Health Insurance Contractual Provisions

While types and levels of health benefits are matters for the employer and insurer to determine, every state regulates certain contractual provisions and requires inclusion of some benefits in group insurance policies. These mandatory provisions tend to be uniform from state to state among insurers, and because of widespread adoption of the National Association of Insurance Commissioners (NAIC) model bills.

Generally, the regulation of contractual provisions focuses on factors such as the grace period, conversion, and incontestability, rather than on factors dealing with the types or levels of benefits. However, in recent years states have required certain minimum health insurance benefits, such as well-baby care and treatment for alcoholism or drug abuse, which must be included in any group health insurance contract. In some states, they must be offered by insurers to employer groups as optional benefits. Mandatory minimum benefits can increase group insurance premiums by an estimated 10% to 20%. Some of these costs can be avoided under an ERISA plan not subject to state regulation.

With few exceptions, the state regulation of contractual provisions affects only those employee benefit plans funded with insurance contracts, and application of ERISA exempts employee benefit plans from most types of state regulation. As a result, states have few laws and regulations that apply to uninsured or self-funded employee benefit plans. However, ERISA does not exempt uninsured plans from state regulation in such areas as age and sex discrimination, and laws pertaining to these areas commonly apply to all benefit plans.

14.1(e): Regulatory Jurisdiction Among States

Group contracts often insure employees living in more than one state. The question of which state laws apply is generally governed under the Doctrine of Comity, by which states recognize within their own territory the laws of other states. A state in which the group contract is delivered to the policyholder generally has governing jurisdiction. The issue of regulatory jurisdiction is complex and varies by type of group plan and agreement.

14.2: Legal Obligations Under Group Health Contracts

Employers' and insurers' legal obligations under group health contracts are determined by the applicable federal or state law in the following areas:

- Coverage eligibility, including dependent eligibility
- Coordination of benefits: determination of primary coverage; determination of benefits payable

- Termination of employment: (1) continuation of coverage under COBRA, requiring an offer of coverage, irrespective of uninsurable health conditions; (2) conversion to an individual policy, irrespective of uninsurable health conditions
- Claims review
- Managed care

14.2(a): Eligibility and Change to New Insurer

Health insurance coverage is rarely available to part-time employees, and contracts typically contain an actively-at-work provision. If an employer changes insurance companies, eligibility requirements generally follow the procedures established by the NAIC Model Regulation on Group Coverage, Discontinuance, and Replacement. This stipulates that coverage will be provided, but possibly limited, under the new contract, to anyone who (1) was covered under the prior contract at the date it was discontinued, and (2) is an eligible classification under the new contract. Employees who actively work on the date coverage is transferred are automatically covered under the new contract and are exempt from any probationary periods.

14.2(b): Dependent Eligibility

The term "dependents" is most commonly defined as "an employee's spouse, who is not legally separated from the employee, and any unmarried children under the age of 19, including stepchildren and adopted children." Coverage is usually provided for children to age 23 if they are full-time students.

14.2(c): Coordination of Benefits

Coordination of benefits is necessary to avoid duplicate coverage which may arise when:

- an employee has two jobs;
- children are covered under both parents' and a step-parent's plans;
- an employee elects coverage under a health plan, even though he/she is covered as a dependent under another plan;
- an individual has coverage under a group plan not provided by an employer, such as children under accident coverage through their school;
- there is coverage under workers' compensation, automobile insurance, or other government-mandated coverages.

To prevent individuals from receiving benefits that exceed actual expenses and to reduce premium, most group plans contain a Coordination of Benefits (COB) provision, under which priorities are established for the payment of benefits by each plan covering the individual. Most COB provisions are based on the 1991 Model Group Coordination of Benefits Regulation, promulgated by the NAIC, which the large majority of states have adopted with some variations.

The COB provisions apply when other coverage exists through group insurance plans, such as Blue Cross/Blue Shield, HMOs, or self-funded plans of another employer. They also apply to workers' compensation, No-Fault automobile insurance benefits, and to coverage for students that is either sponsored or provided by educational institutions. They typically do not, and cannot in most states, apply to coverages provided under individual health insurance policies purchased outside the employment relationship.

14.2(d): Continuation of Coverage Under COBRA

The Federal Consolidated Omnibus Budget Reconciliation Act of 1985 (COBRA), and some state laws, requires that group health plans allow employees and certain beneficiaries to elect to have their current health insurance extended at group rates for 18 months, (36 months for certain beneficiaries), following a qualifying event that results in loss of coverage, if they elect to pay up to 102% of the group premium. COBRA applies only to employers that had 20 or more employees on a typical business day during the preceding calendar year. Church and government plans are exempt, but may offer similar coverage extensions.

Failure to comply with the Act can result in an excise tax of up to $100/day for each person denied coverage, and employers have been sued by uninsured former employees. The tax can be levied on the employer or on the insurer entity that administers the benefits. A "qualifying event" includes death of the covered employee, termination, including quitting, retiring or being fired, or reduction in hours, for any reason other than gross misconduct. Coverage extends to spouses or children after divorce, separation or employee's eligibility for Medicare, and a child's ceasing to be an eligible dependent under the plan. Any beneficiary, employee, spouse, or dependent who loses coverage because of a qualifying event can elect continued coverage without providing evidence of insurability. The beneficiary must be allowed to continue identical coverage provided to active employees or dependents.

IRS enforces COBRA through the Technical and Miscellaneous Revenue Act of 1988 (TAMRA). IRS auditors typically ask for: a copy of employer's procedural manual, form letter, and group health plans, statistical information on the requested tax years, a narrative of procedures, and documentation demonstrating compliance. If the auditor finds that the employer acted with reasonable cause and incorporated proper COBRA procedures under TAMRA--COBRA training, written administration instructions, a program designed and updated on competent professional advice and an outside program monitor--IRS may waive any penalties if the employer complies within 30 days. If IRS finds the employer acted with "willful neglect", the penalty is $100 per day, or $200 per day for a family, multiplied by the number of days of failure to comply. To stay out of court and avoid IRS penalties, employers should remember these principles:

(1) Mandatory procedures, including proper notification and notice language, adherence to COBRA time frames, and consistency in applying its provisions. (No special coverage favors for friends.)

(2) A qualified beneficiary under COBRA must be covered.

(3) The active employee determines who gets insurance coverage.

(4) All qualified beneficiaries have independent coverage, independent of anyone else in their family, and have all the rights of active employees--plus some. They can make

available moves within the plan, and can sometimes unbundle coverage that active employees cannot.

(5) Always give the benefit of the doubt in a gray area of COBRA to the qualified beneficiary to avoid mistakes and help your business stay out of court.

(6) Independent contractors do not become qualified beneficiaries so it is important to follow procedures to assure they are independent contractors for out-sourcing work, and not employees.

14.2(e): Tort Claims Underlie Both Group Health and W.C. Benefits

Injured employees and others bring tort claims after medical and loss of income benefits are paid, seeking additional damages or compensation. W.C. insurers and health plans also seek recovery of benefits paid from negligent third parties through coordination of benefits, other insurance, and subrogation provisions. Although billions are paid in w.c. first-party no-fault benefits annually, from a legal perspective this is an island in the broader sea of tort recovery.[6] Tort recovery is available to workers who have received w.c. benefits, and to employers' health benefit plans. These tort claims are outlined below.

Applicable Law	State W.C. Law	State/Fed Tort Law
Benefit Agreements	W.C. Stat. Benefits	Employers Liability

EMPLOYEE WELFARE PLANS
FEDERAL ERISA PLANS

Medical Plans	Disability Plans	Other Plans
	STD	
	LTD	
	Leaves	

Initial Claims	"No Fault" Pmt	Third Party
Underlying liability	3rd Party sub. and cob. w/s.s.	Dual Capac'y inten'l torts fellow empl. employ. pract. liability discrimination, harassment, wrongful hiring, promotion, dismissal, ada

FIRST PARTY

COB/AUTO/WC	COB/AUTO/WC
3RD PARTY	3RD PARTY
TORT SUBROGATION	TORT SUBROGATION

14.3: Coordinating Workers' Compensation, Employer Liability, and Benefit Plan Liability Insurance

An employee files a workers' comp claim on January 1, 1990 for injuries caused by a fellow employee's sexual assault and after receiving w.c. benefits, subsequently resigns in February, 1992. The claimant promptly files a suit against the employer and fellow employees, alleging a retaliatory campaign of slander in front of other employees, and defamation in performance appraisals, leading her to quit employment to escape harassment and intolerable working conditions. Upon resignation, her request for severance payments was denied by administrators of the benefits plan, and she did not elect COBRA-required continuation of health insurance. The complaint alleges constructive and wrongful discharge[7], intentional and negligent infliction of emotional distress[8], defamation[9], arbitrary and capricious denial of benefits due under an ERISA-governed plan[10], and failure to offer continuing coverage under the HMO plan clinic in her home town.

14.3(a): Review All Employer Liability Policies for Coverage

The allegations in this one claimant case set the stage for the employer to review the following liability policies for potential defense and indemnity coverage of employment-related claims:

- The Commercial General Liability (CGL) Policy with Personal Injury coverage
- The "Employers' Liability" portion of the Workers' Compensation (WC) Policy
- The Directors and Officers (D&O) Liability Policy
- The Excess and Umbrella Liability Policies
- The Benefit Plan Administration Liability Policy
- The Employee Benefit Fiduciary Liability Policy
- The Employment Practices Liability Policy

Other aspects of liability insurance review are presented in Chapter 16, Risk Management, Section 16.4.

14.3(b): First Review Liability Policies for Defense Coverage

Both the employer and fellow employees seek insurance coverage of defense costs. Generally, insurers must defend employment claims if the complaint allegations are within the scope of the policy coverage. However, employers may seek a court's ruling when insurers decline defense coverage. In a sexual harassment case, an insurer accepted defense because allegations of defamation were within the scope of coverage. When the court dismissed the defamation claim, the insurer withdrew its defense coverage. Then, upon the employer's request, a Minnesota court held the insurer still had a duty to defend and awarded attorneys' fees to the employer. An appellate court agreed, finding that the allegations of "bodily injury" remained and there was no evidence the employer intended to create a hostile work environment. The court identified several allegations of conduct outside "the scope of employment" which are not subject to the employment exclusions in the insurance policy.[11] Whether there is defense coverage for the fellow employee depends on whether employees are included as insureds under the liability policy and whether fellow-employee claims are excluded from coverage.

14.3(c): CGL Lacks Employment Claim Coverage

The employer's CGL policies for the years 1990 through 1995 should be reviewed, but coverage is limited for the allegations raised in this one claimant case noted above. Both the "workers' compensation" and "employer's liability" exclusions in CGL Coverage A serve to remove coverage for those allegations on the basis that risks are better covered elsewhere.

However, the broad language excluding bodily injury to an employee . . . "arising out of and in the course of employment" will likely exclude some risks that are not within the plain meaning of the workers' compensation and employer's liability coverage. Those risks may not be insurable in the standard market.[12] The exclusions in CGL Coverage B of personal injury "arising out of the willful violation of a penal statute or ordinance committed by or with the consent of the insured" excludes a risk that may be relevant in some employment claims.[13]

The ISO "Employment-related Practices Exclusion" endorsement (10/93 Ed.) amends both coverage A and B, attempting to remove most employment litigation from the scope of basic coverage provided by the CGL policy. With this endorsement, employers must purchase employment practices liability coverage either by endorsement to the CGL policy, or in a separate policy in the surplus lines specialty market.[14] Insurers have been successful in enforcing these exclusions.[15]

14.3(d)(1): Workers' Compensation Shields Employer Against Sexual Harassment Claims

If sexual assault or rape claims are considered "on-the-job" injury, subject to workers' compensation, the injured employee's tort claim against the employer would likely be dismissed.

The employer's W.C. and Employer's Liability policy should be reviewed when the employer asserting exclusivity of workers' comp seeks a dismissal of the employee's civil action for the employee's emotional distress injuries. See Chapter 16 Section 16.4(f)(4).

In spite of this w.c. exclusivity shield, defending the sexual assault/rape tort claim can be costly. In a recent case, a former employee of Saks Fifth Avenue sued Saks for $10 million, claiming it was negligence in hiring a convicted rapist as a security guard and in ignoring her complaints and those of other women, that lead to his raping her on the job. First, a w.c. administration law judge must decide if it can be settled within the workers' comp system, thereby precluding the tort claim. If either side disagrees with the judge's ruling, this New York case is placed before three commissioners on the State W.C. Review Board. If either side disagrees with the Review Board's decision, they can take the case before all 13 W.C. Board Commissioners. If the case is still contested, the w.c. Board decision could be appealed into the state civil court system. There is legal precedent for cases like this to be held "work-related". Therefore, the employee's tort claim would be dismissed.

14.3(d)2: Workers' Compensation Plus Lawsuit Recovery

An employee is entitled to workers' comp benefits as the exclusive remedy from the employer. However, the injured employee may also sue a third party. The third party cannot generally shift the portion of its liability back to a negligent employer since the exclusive remedy under the Workers' Compensation Act (WCA) prevents tort liability arising out of employee accidents.[16] See Chapter 16, Section 16.4(f)(4) for discussion of employers' liability for job-connected harassment and violence.

Other liability policies should be reviewed--officers and directors, benefit plan administration liability, benefit plan fiduciary liability policies, and, finally, excess and umbrella policies.

14.3(e): Directors and Officers Liability Policy

This insurance policy may provide coverage for a disgruntled employee's claim against individual corporate officials. A D & O policy generally indemnifies the company for claims premised on wrongful acts of officers and directors, and they also insure directors and officers personally.

14.3(f): Employee Benefit Plan Liability Insurance

An Employee Benefit Plan Liability insurance policy typically applies to the administration of one or more of the following types of plans or insurance:

1. Group life insurance or group accident and health insurance;
2. Profit-sharing plans, pension plans, retirement plans, or employee stock subscription plans;
3. Workers' compensation, unemployment insurance, salary continuation plans, social security benefits, or disability benefits insurance;
4. Travel plans, savings plans, or vacation plans; or
5. Any other type of insurance or plan described in the policy schedule.

The policy usually states it will pay all sums which an insured becomes legally obligated to pay as damages due to injury to an employee caused by negligent act, error, or omission of the insured in the administration of an employee benefit program.

"Administration" as defined in the policy, means performing the following acts for the employee benefit program:

1. Giving counsel to employees;
2. Interpreting the employee benefit program;
3. Handling and maintenance;
4. Affecting enrollment or termination of employees;
5. Calculating service and compensation credits;
6. Calculating benefits;
7. Preparing employee communication material, reports required by government agencies, and reports concerning participants' benefits;
8. Processing claims; and
9. Collection of contributions and distribution thereof.

The policy typically covers defense costs, including alternative dispute resolution proceedings, but there is no coverage for the following:

1. Any dishonest, fraudulent, criminal or malicious act, libel, slander, discrimination, or humiliation.
2. Bodily injury or property damage.
3. Failure to perform a contract by any insurer, including the failure of any plan included in the employee benefit program.
4. The insured's failure to comply with any law concerning workers' compensation, unemployment insurance, social security, or disability benefits.
5. a. The failure of any stock, bond, or mutual fund or other investment, to perform as represented;

  b. Advice given by an insured to participate or not to participate in stock subscription plan; or

  c. Investment or non-investment of funds.

6. Violation of responsibilities, obligations, or duties imposed on fiduciaries by the Employment Retirement Income Security Act of 1974, as amended, and any regulations pertaining thereto.

7. Claims resulting from the termination of any plan included in the employee benefit program.

14.3(g): Pension and Welfare Fund Fiduciary Liability Policies

These insurance policies cover pension and welfare plans, administrators, and trustees, against suits alleging wrongful acts in the operation of such plans.

Exclusion 6 in the administration liability policy creates the need for an Employee Fiduciary Liability policy to cover breach of ERISA fiduciary standards. The standards are outlined in Section 15.3, 15.4, 15.5 and 15.10 of Chapter 15. Both benefit administration liability coverage and fiduciary liability coverage are available in one insurance policy.

Given the broad preempted effect of ERISA, many employment-related complaints amount to claims based on rights under ERISA.[17] Because remedies under ERISA are narrowly construed by courts, a fiduciary responsibility insurance policy may respond to defend claims, but it is unlikely to pay claims for the amount of employee benefits awarded to a successful claimant. A claimant employee often will only be awarded wrongfully withheld benefits, which are outside the scope of the covered losses.[18]

Excess and umbrella liability policies and any employment practices liability policies should be reviewed for potential coverage of employment disputes.[19]

14.4: Managed Health Care and Liability

Managed health care means that within a medical expense or disability benefit or w.c. plan, the behavior and choices of patients and care providers are directed to contain costs. At one extreme, traditional insurance plans require second opinions and/or hospital pre-certification. At the other extreme, managed health plans such as Health Maintenance Organizations (HMOs) limit a participant's choice of medical providers, negotiate provider fees, and use case assessment.

Generally, the greater the degree of managed care, the lower the costs. Traditional plans with little managed care cost the most, and closed panel HMOs generally cost the least. Surveys suggest that participant satisfaction is high among all types of health plans and, surprisingly, slightly higher for managed care plans. Further, the rate of cost increase in traditional plans continues to exceed increases in managed care plans. Although the average annual rate of increases for health benefit premiums has declined in recent years, the rate of increase still exceeds the general inflation rate, the medical inflation rate, and the non-supervisory workers' rate of earnings increase.

14.4(a): Managed Care in Health Plans Creates Liability

When patient and care provider choices are directed, managed care creates potential liability for employers, managed care organizations (MCOs) and medical care providers. New claims allege employers and MCOs wrongfully restricted care which was covered under employee benefit health plans, and medical providers are subject to claims for failure to follow directives of patients and their families.

Recent court rulings indicate MCOs can be held vicariously liable for actions of their physician contractors. This liability and the growth of physician organizations like physician hospital organizations (HPOs) and independent practice associations (IPAs) increase the need for professional liability insurance to cover managed care organizations.

Two insureds enrolled in an employer-sponsored health plan sought damages as a result of the actions of physicians who contracted with an HMO. These were employee benefit plans subject to ERISA which preempted state medical malpractice regulations. However, two courts ruled that the ERISA exemption did not extend to the vicarious liability of an HMO.[20] Each case was remanded back to its respective state for consideration under state malpractice guidelines. "If the issue was malpractice between a doctor and a patient, rather than the administration of a plan, then the state malpractice law is not preempted by ERISA."

14.4(b): Liability Insurance for Managed Care Organizations

A managed care organization's (MCO's) vicarious liability relates to provider services administered by physicians that contract with the MCO, which places direct liability from utilization review and credentialing, unless it contracts its services out, in which case it could face an exposure to vicarious liability. An MCO can also be held vicariously liable in medical case management and quality assurance areas.

Some medical liability insurance companies provide vicarious liability coverage to insureds, with certain exceptions under its physician and surgeon professional liability policy. Separate Errors & Omissions and Directors & Officers liability policies are available with this professional liability coverage. The professional liability and D & O for managed care products combines direct and vicarious liability coverage with E & O.

There has not been sufficient time for the law to settle how liability and damages will be allocated to these entities and/or direct providers. Some PHOs, IPAs, and other physician organizations have formed limited liability companies which need this professional liability coverage. This professional health care liability coverage combines vicarious and direct liability for malpractice exposures and business E & O coverage. Medical malpractice insurance companies have had to adopt underwriting to reflect these changes in health care and the integration of physicians and hospitals.[21]

14.4(c): Workers' Compensation and Managed Care

Under the workers' compensation statutes, some states now apply certain managed care techniques, including provider payment under fee schedules' relative value substitute for 85% prevailing charges; controlling utilization of provider services; specifying medical treatment protocols; explicitly permitting employer-paid deductibles; removal of benefit integration obstacles; and use of light duty pools.

Applications of managed care techniques to workers' comp can save medical costs and improved health care. A savings of nearly 5% is estimated through reduced utilization, which is reducing the number of treatments, using less expensive services, and using fee discounts. In states like Minnesota, employers and insurers who contract with managed care organizations are required to compensate medical providers using the statutory relative value fee schedule. A 5% to 15% savings is estimated in fee discounts, paying fee schedules rather than individual fee-for-service. A study by Milliman & Robertson estimated savings in administrative costs and medical costs between 7% and 20%. (9/14/95)

Some states have certified managed care organizations (MCOs), a network of healthcare providers in a managed care system, to treat outpatient and non-occupational injuries. Today, a high portion of all employees in states like California and Minnesota receive medical treatment for work-related injuries from managed care organizations.[22] Using an early intervention "managed care" format for workers' compensation, research finds savings of 23% to 27% per claim through aggressive case management.[23]

14.5: 24-Hour Coverage: Coordinating Workers' Compensation and Health Insurance Benefits

While all employers must satisfy the state mandate to provide workers' compensation (w.c.) insurance, many employers also provide off-the-job group health and disability coverages. Coordination begins with the benefit similarities of these two systems.

Employee Benefits	Workers Compensation
Medical coverage	Medical Coverage
Short term disability	Temporary disability
Long term disability	Permanent disability
Life Insurance	Death Benefit
Accidental death/dismemberment	Death Benefit
ADA accommodation	Vocational Rehabilitation
Return to life function	Return to work initiatives

Twenty-four hour health care programs combine medical benefits for occupational and non-occupational injuries and illnesses. Under the 24-hour care approach, insurers provide employers an insurance option combining state required workers' compensation coverage and managed care group health into a single benefit that participating employers may offer employees on a voluntary basis. The major goals of this coverage are to increase continuity of care for workers' compensation claimants and to lower the overall costs of medical and injury claims.

Several possible types of 24-hour coverage have been described by the National Association of Insurance Commissioners (N.A.I.C.): marketing the product, medical coverage only, disability coverage only, coverage of accidents only, coverage of diseases only, and coverage of medical and disability.[24] Benefits coordination means consideration of both on-job and off-job employee health or treatment in any aspect of benefits management--marketing, pricing, financing, or claims administration. Today, employers can obtain the following elements of coordination.

- buy coverages from one brokerage source which provides w.c., disability and medical insurance under separate policies. Although one policy covering all these benefits is not currently available, the number of insurers and vendors can be reduced, e.g., use one reinsurer on both w.c. and group health excess coverage.

- use the same managed healthcare provider network for both off and on-the-job medical and income loss benefits.

- use the same benefits administration unit for claims processing, a nurse line, case management, or information system collection and reporting. A doubtful w.c claim can be paid promptly under the medical plan, and later, an internal funds transfer can be made to w.c. if the claim is determined to be job-connected.

- use managed medical and disability claims administration which addresses both on-the-job and off-the-job claims' records.

- use a single case management team for occupational and non-occupational injuries, comprised of a nurse, benefits manager, attorney, and plant safety person.

- use a single claims notice and benefits access point for both off-job and on-the-job injuries.

- use a common database or at least computers which "talk" to one another to coordinate eligibility data, claims history and coverage data. In the future, completely integrated systems will likely generate management reports, utilization/performance details of care providers in group health, w.c., vocational rehabilitation, social security monitoring and retrospective, bill reduction reports; also in the future is electronic data interchange from physicians' offices on all of these benefits.

These aspects of coordinated benefits must be customized to each group's circumstances. The best candidates for complete benefits coordination are large groups (over 900 eligible employees), self-funded in both state w.c. and health benefits, under an ERISA plan, with sophisticated benefits administration, and a long-term commitment from top management.

Potential advantages from 24-hour benefits coordination include control over escalating medical and disability income costs, reduced administrative costs, increased continuity of care, increased control over health care delivery, and avoidance of duplicate payments for the same medical income loss. There are, however, a number of legislative, institutional, and regulatory barriers to complete integration of 24-hour coverage.

14.5(a): State Activity in 24-Hour Coverage

Complete 24-hour coverage is far from a market-wide reality. However, a number of states allow various forms of 24-hour coverage.

Eighteen states, including Minnesota, allow various forms of alternative coverages. These alternative coverages to the workers' compensation statutory benefits do not provide 24-hour coverage products but permit modification in the workers' comp delivery system, including managed care. The states typically require that workers' comp benefits be greater than or equal to those required under the Workers' Compensation Act (WCA) and require regulatory approval.

Seven states, California, Florida, Georgia, Kentucky, Maine, Oregon, and Washington, currently have 24-hour coverage pilot programs. These states have approved or are considering approval of private entities offering 24-hour coverage products.

Colorado, Hawaii, Iowa and Oklahoma are currently studying or considering 24-hour coverage. Three other states, Massachusetts, Montana and North Carolina, have conducted studies and concluded that 24-hour coverage was not appropriate at the time.

In New Jersey, South Carolina and Texas, where workers' compensation laws are elective for most employers, employers can opt out of the current workers' compensation system. However, Texas is the only state where there has been significant opting-out activity with 40% of the market electing to opt-out, define their own job-connected benefits, and be exposed to tort claims by insured employees.

Several models of benefits coordination are proceeding in many states:

1. To date, sixteen employer and labor groups in 8 states, including New York, Kentucky, Florida, California and Minnesota, have formed collectively-bargained workers' compensation managed care delivery programs under the "Bechtel Amendment", enacted since 1990. (Minnesota enacted in 1995, included in MS 176.1812) Certain employers and unions are authorized to make changes in the non-benefit aspects of workers' compensation collectively bargained agreements. The following changes in workers' compensation benefit delivery are examples:

   a. An alternative dispute resolution system.
   b. A network of healthcare providers.
   c. A list of impartial positions for expert opinions.
   d. A light-duty return-to-work program.
   e. A network of occupational rehabilitation and retraining providers.
   f. Safety committees.

These types of modifications and the workers' comp delivery system are intended to decrease overall costs and improve delivery of benefits and services by reducing litigation, increasing the speed of dispute resolution, and eliminating conflicting medical and vocational opinions that delay appropriate treatment and return to work. New opportunities of w.c. and health benefit coordination arise when these plans are governed by the same people, or trustees, or employers, who govern employee health benefits.

2. Some HMO's, Blue Cross/Blue Shield plans, and insurance companies are marketing small group health plans and workers' compensation benefits.

3. Some large employers have joined coalitions to integrate group health and workers' compensation benefits.

4. Some state governments administer group health plans and are beginning to coordinate workers' compensation benefits.

14.5(b): 24-Hour Coverage Cost Control

Twenty-four hour coverage can reduce litigation and litigation costs.[25] Improved administration, prompt claims payment, and better communication with injured employees and care providers tend to reduce legal actions, particularly in workers' comp. By using a single payer, litigation on the question of whether the injury was work-connected is reduced, and litigation between workers' comp and health insurers can be reduced. For example, FHP Int'l Co. had legal and medical costs substantially decrease due to reduced litigation using 24-hour medical coverage coordination.[26]

14.5(b)(1): Explicit Plan Standards Can Reduce Litigation Costs

Both ERISA and workers' compensation laws can be used to reduce employer litigation cost by incorporating explicit claims decision criteria. Litigation costs can be reduced by carefully drafting benefit plan documents to explicitly grant discretionary authority to plan administrators, and by explicitly stating claim review standards. This permits courts to defer to the decisions of plan administrators rather than engaging in a de novo review and possible trial on the issues. Litigation can be reduced if the plan document grants the administrator the following types of authority:

- to determine eligibility for benefits
- to construe plan terms
- to determine need for treatment in advance
- to apply the requirements of "medical necessity" or "reasonable charges" or prevailing charge to apply experimental care or custodial care, or medical emergency provisions

When the authority is explicitly granted, and the plan document standards are applied by the administrator, courts are likely to defer to plan administrator claims denial decisions, and focus narrowly on the question of whether the denial was "arbitrary-and-capricious" or an "abuse-of-discretion", rather than subject the administrator's decision to a de novo review.[27]

Just as providing explicit claim decision standards reduces litigation costs in health plans under ERISA, managed care standards have been applied in w.c. to reduce costs. To control medical costs, in 1992 the Minnesota legislature replaced the medical fee schedule with a relative value-based schedule and developed a managed care plan option for employers. In June, 1994, the Minnesota Department of Labor and Industry promulgated explicit rules relating to w.c. treatment parameters. There are general rules for medical imaging, emergency hospitalization and surgery, and specific rules for diagnosis and treatment for low-back pain and upper extremity disorders. Prior authorization from the insurer is required, and post-operative therapy is limited, among many other explicit standards.[28] Ironically, these rules produced litigation which successfully challenged the rules which the Commissioner of the Department of Labor and Industry contends are essential to accomplish the legislative goal of cost containment.

The Supreme Court of Minnesota held, among other things, that the rules infringe on the discretionary power of the compensation judge. "We also think it important that the legislature asked for 'standards' and 'criteria' for judging the propriety of medical care, not regulations on the delivery of care. With standards come flexibility and the recognition that a certain amount of medical judgment is necessary in providing adequate and reasonable medical care . . . and that a certain amount of judicial discretion is likewise required in deciding whether care is compensable."[29]

14.5(b)(2): Coordination Reduces Costs

Under 24-hour coverage, the doctor/patient relationship is expected to improve with the quality of care. Employees should have improved access to medical care and doctors won't worry about who is going to pay and can focus on needed treatment. There can be little or no restriction for pre-existing conditions; a short or non-existent waiting period before benefits become available to new employees; and few limitations on dollar amount or coverage, or types of services. Since workers' comp claims are defined as the "occurrence of an injury during the policy period" and group health insurance claims are defined as "a provision of services during the policy period", a complete, but currently unavailable, 24-hour coverage plan would cover full future costs of all medical benefits associated with a work-related injury.

If cost sharing through deductibles or co-payments becomes a part of workers' comp, as it currently is in the group medical, substantial cost reductions are possible. An $80 million health insurance experiment conducted by the Rand Corporation found that participants in a health insurance plan with 25% co-insurance rate spent about 20% less on health care than did patients who received free medical care. Minnesota data suggests that co-insurance could reduce the consumption of health care by injured workers, if the workers who wanted extensive care for back disorders would share part of the cost. (Burton, John F., Jr.)

Since workers' comp laws do not permit cost sharing, we do not know how well can workers' comp healthcare costs be managed without the use of cost-sharing techniques. Research findings indicate mixed results for treatment of w.c. lower back pain. Orthopedic surgery and chiropractic treatment produced negative results with longer loss time periods, but physical therapy produced positive results, shortening return-to-work periods.[30]

Coordinating the medical coverages can reduce claims administration costs associated with "double-dipping", the filing of claims for the same injury under both workers' comp and the employee benefits plan. Employers can reduce medical costs, eliminate duplicate bills, pursue excess and fraud, and reduce corporate administration costs. A Milliman & Robertson study estimated savings from the elimination of "double dipping" at 2-5%.[31] Using only one utilization management program for benefits, instead of separate programs for workers' comp and group health, can reduce staff time spent on administrative functions.

The greatest long-term savings potential is derived by applying aggressive w.c. return-to-work (rtw) strategies to non-occupational return-to-life function disability. All loss time is very expensive in both direct claims paid and hidden costs from being off the job. For every $100 in disability benefits paid, employers may pay $700 for temporaries, overtime, training or recruiting, plus loss of business. RTW strategies applied to disability plans can save 30% to 40% of non-occupational claim expenses. Finally, allowing uniform use of certain managed care techniques, including preferred provider networks, can increase savings. E.g., not permitting healthcare providers to vary charges for the same injury between workers' comp and group insurance may reduce costs.[32]

14.5(c): Does 24-Hour Coverage Benefit Your Company?

Answers to the following questions will help determine whether your company might benefit from coordinating workers' comp and group health insurance.

1. Do you offer group health coverage to employees? If your answer is no, there is no opportunity for coordination.

However, it may be beneficial to provide employee education and training on workers' compensation benefits and how to best utilize those benefits, as well as other medical insurance benefits which may be available to employees, such as under automobile policies and health policies of a spouse.

2. What type of health benefits are provided to the employee group--ranging from additional major medical insurance through broader HMO-managed care coverages? The broader HMO-type benefits with no limits, few or no copayments, and few or low deductibles, are closer to the complete no-limit, no-deductible, no-copay workers' comp medical benefits.

3. What opportunities for coordination are available in your marketplace? Is it possible to use the same medical provider for employees on-the-job and off-the-job medical care? Are the available medical care providers attuned to both occupational and non-occupational medical practices and return-to-function, as well as return-to-work programs? Is a single claims administrator available to coordinate claims records for both workers' comp and group medical, which would make it easier to coordinate on-and-off-the-job benefits administration and claims?

4. Do you offer wage-loss benefits for sick leave, family leave, short or long-term disability? If you do, the same questions listed above should be applied. In addition, the following questions should be answered.

5. To what extent is managed care applied in workers' comp, wage loss, and to what extent is managed care applied to non-workers' comp wage loss benefits?

6. What is workers' comp cost as a percentages of payroll, what is group health as a percentage of payroll, and what is wage loss benefits as a percentage of payroll?

7. What is the medical/wage loss profile of your employees? A high utilization, high average age, high risk employee profile offers greater potential cost advantages from benefit coordination and certain HMOs, Blue Cross/Blue Shield plans may offer much lower premiums to your group because they base premiums on a community-wide average cost.

8. Has your company established a "case management team", including a nurse, an attorney, an occupational specialist, a human resources person, and a risk manager? Variations of this type of team approach to benefits coordination and managed care have successfully improved benefits and reduced costs.

9. Does an occupational nurse immediately contact any employee when short-term disability begins, irrespective of whether the disability is a workers' comp or non-workers' comp claim? Is the information on the diagnosis of the injury or illness provided to the claims administrators? Is a return-to-life function communication system in place to include the employee, occupational nurse, treating physicians and supervisors?

Exploring answers to these questions with your broker, counsel, or consultant, may lead to reduced cost and improved benefits.

14.5(d): Employment and ADA Claims Prevention

Employers should not ask job applicants about disabilities. They should ask only job-related questions about ability to perform a specific job function. Employers should not give medical exams unless required by the job functions, and should not ask about things such as drug addiction, work-related injury, or sick leave.

Employers can ask if an applicant will need a "reasonable accommodation" in the workplace to perform the job function. Under ADA a "reasonable accommodation" is "a modification or adjustment to a job, work environment, or a way of doing things that enables a disabled person to enjoy equal employment opportunities."

Employers should avoid making promises, implying that employment is on anything other than an "at-will" basis. Absent an express or implied term as to duration, an employment relationship is terminable "at-will" by either party.

Any criticism of employees should be reduced to writing to avoid the cases when an employer is defended in a wrongful dismissal claim and the employer has, all along, checked a box stating that the employee who has been fired, has been "meeting all expectations of his job."

Employers should impress upon supervisors that they are representatives of the company; that their acts can make the employer liable and make them liable, too.

Employment practice areas should be subject to an audit: Employment applications, re-employment inquiries, interview forms, standard-form job-offer letters, and legally required postings, employee codes of conduct, employee handbooks, evaluation forms, standard-form employment contracts, and Occupational Health & Safety Act audits.

Other areas that should be examined include training programs, including those concerned with sexual harassment, discrimination and OSHA, termination procedures, Consolidated Omnibus Budget Reconciliation Act compliance, integration audits, standard forms of separation and severance agreements, and Family Medical Leave Act (FMLA) and ADA anti-harassment policies and procedures.[33]

14.6: Tips to Control Health Plan Costs and Liability

1. Identify the federal or state law applicable to your employee health plan and review its standards for compliance.
2. Review availability of health plans to select those which best fit your employee's needs in terms of the following:
    a. Healthcare providers interested in and able to serve your employee's occupational and non-occupational medical care needs.
    b. The best education and training process for employees on benefits available, and best paths to using the system services.

c. Health insurers with existing employee groups whose health care utilization is less than your employee population, since a portion of the average pool claims costs are typically included in all insurer premiums.
   d. Have a managed care framework satisfactory to your employees.
   e. Identify and communicate costs of medical treatment to patients so employees know the actual costs and can help audit the system.
   f. Contract with the health plan organization arranging a 3 to 5-year pricing and service relationship.
3. Careful and regular communication of plan benefits coverage limitations, employees' responsibilities, and care providers responsibilities.
4. Prompt communication and care provider assistance to injured employees and their families, explaining how to best use the services, what to expect, and the employees' responsibilities. Occupational nursing services to immediately work with injured employees and doctors are generally a good investment, and prompt the best managed care and return-to-function goals. Small gestures yield fast return-to-work -- get well cards, flowers, regular phone calls, and transportation to and from the doctor -- a $35 cab fare might save thousands in lost time. Eliminate all return-to-work disincentives. Total off-the-job, after-tax payments should be less than on-the-job, after-tax salary. Be sure W.C. plus non-occupational disability benefits are lower and be sure workers' comp payments are offset by pension, social security and other payments.
5. Have a liability exposure audit and compare the results with all your liability insurance policies -- from the employer's liability

portion of your workers' compensation policy to your employment practices liability policies.
6. Effective communication among all parties leads to improved services, utilization, and will reduce liability exposures.

1. Adapted from "Benefits Costs Dip for Many Employers", J. Geisel, Business Insurance, Dec. 4, 1995, p. 1.

2. Earlier decisions appear to interpret ERISA as restricting a broad range of state provisions that may relate to employer health plans, but the most recent U.S. Supreme Court decision noted that "Nothing in the language of the (Employment Retirement Security) . . . indicates that Congress chose to displace general health care regulation." This may suggest greater flexibility for state regulation.

3. Lockheed Corp. v. Spink, No. 95-809, U.S. Sup. Ct., June 10, 1996 citing Curtiss-Wright Corp. v. Schoonejongen, 514 U.S. ("Employers and plan sponsors can amend a welfare benefit plan or a pension plan without violating ERISA's 'prohibited transactions' section 406(a)(1)(D), described in Section 15.10(b) of Chapter 15, Pension Plan Liability.

4. The Supreme Court decision in Firestone Tire & Rubber Co. v. Bruch, (1989) 489 US 101, 103 L. Ed.2d 80, 109 S. Ct. 948, 10 EBC 1873.

5. Annotation Judicial Review of Denial of Health Care Benefits Under Employee Benefit Plan Governed by Employee Retirement Income Security Act (ERISA) 29USCS@1132(a)(1)(B) Post-Firestone cases. Michael A. de Freitas, J.D., adopted from 128 A.L.R. Fed. 1.

6. Adopted from "Workers' Compensation and Product Liability: The Interaction of a Tort and a Non-Tort Regime", Paul C. Weiler, Ohio State Law Journal, Fall 1989, 50 Ohio State L.J. 825.

7. E.g. defamation under a theory of self-publication. See Lewis v. Equit. Life Assur. Soc'y, 389 N.W.2d 876 (Minn. 1986).

8. See e.g. Wilson v. Monarch Paper Co., 939 F.2d 1138 (5th Cir. 1991). An employee can state a viable claim against the employer for slander with regard to statements made to fellow

employees and also might state a claim for defamation with respect to performance appraisals under the theory of self-publication. Lewis v. Equitable Life Assurance Soc'y, 389 N.W.2d 876.

9. See Lewis, supra.

10. Adapted from "Principles of Insurance Coverage: A Guide for the Employment Lawyer", Francis J. Mootz, 18 W. New Eng. Law Review 5, 1996. Notes come from FN. 20 in the article. 29 USC 1132 (a)(1)(B)(1988) but if the plan accords discretionary powers to the administrator to determine eligibility for benefits, the court may reverse an administrator's denial of benefits only if it is found to be arbitrary or capricious; Firestone Tire & Rubber Co. v. Bruch, 489 U.S. 101 (1989).

11. Meadowbrook, Inc. v. Tower Ins. Co., 543 N.W.2d 418 (Minn. App. 1996).

12. Ottumwa Hous. Auth. v. State Farm Fire & Cas. Co., 495 N.W.2d 723, 727 (Iowa 1993).

13. MGM v. Liberty Mut. Ins. Co., 855 P.2d 77, 80 (Can. 1993) (enforcing exclusion by denying coverage to an employer that subjected its employees to wiretaps that were illegal under the Federal Criminal Code).

14. Machson v. Montelteone, 711-13.

15. Transamerica Ins. Co. v. Superior Court, 35 Cal. Rptr.2d 259 (1994) (exclusions in Workers' Compensation and Employers' Liability Policy), reh'd denied, 40 Cal. Rptr.2d 808 (1995); Teague Motor Co. v. Federated Serv. Ins. Co., 869 P.2d 1130 (Wash. Ct. App. 1994) (exclusion of employment discrimination from umbrella policy); Old Republic Ins. Co. v. Comprehensive Health Care Assoc., Inc., 2 F.3d 105 (5th Cir. 1993) (enforcing "sexual abuse" exclusion and "employment-related claim" exclusion in CGL policy and enforcing an "employment" exclusion in umbrella policy); Reliable Springs Co. v. St. Paul Fire & Marine Ins. Co., 869 F.2d 993 (6th Cir.

1989) (enforcing "discrimination and unfair employment practices" exclusion).

16. "Once is Enough: A Proposed Bar of the Injured Employee's Cause of Action Against a Third Party", Phillip D. Oliver, 58 Fordham L. Rev. 117 (Nov. 1989).

17. See e.g. Ingersoll-Rand Co. v. McClendon, 498 U.S. 133 (1989); Sanson v. General Motors Corp., 966 F.2d 618, 621 (11th Cir. 1992) Cert. denied, 113 S. Ct. 1578 (1993) (holding that the plaintiff employees' state law claims were preempted by ERISA, even though ERISA afforded no relief for the alleged wrongdoing).

18. See Mass. Mut. Life Ins. Co. v. Russell, 473 U.S. 134 (1985) and its developing progeny. If developing federal common law actions of equitable estoppel survive Supreme Court scrutiny, it may be that a suit for promised benefits, admittedly outside the scope of the unambiguous plan language, will trigger fiduciary liability coverage. See e.g. Black v. TIC Ind. Corp., 90 F 2d 112, 114-15 (7th Cir. 1990).

19. See e.g. Josten's Inc. v. Northfield Ins. Co., 527 N.W.2d 116 (Minn. Ct. App. 1995); Dixon Dist. Co. v. Hanover Ins. Co., 641 N.E.2d 395 (Ill. 1994); Teague Motor Co. v. Federated Cerv. Ins. Co., 869 P.2d 1130 (Wash. Ct. App. 1994); Clark-Peterson Co. v. Independent Ins. Assoc. Ltd., 492 N.W.2d 675 (Iowa 1992).

20. Dukes v. U.S. Healthcare, 3rd U.S. Cir. Ct. Appeals, June 1995, and Pacific Care of Oklahoma, Inc. v. Burrage, 10th U.S. Cir. Ct. Appeals, July 1995.

21. Adopted from "Court Rulings from New Liability Plan Development", John Niedzielski, Nat'l. Underwriter, May 13, 1996.

22. Tompkins, Neville C. "Action at the State Level: A New Round of Workers' Compensation Controls." Compensation and Benefits Review, May/June 1995, p. 45(2).

23. Bowling, M., "Measuring the Financial Impact of Workers' Compensation Managed Care Techniques", J. of W.C., Spring, 38-47, 1996.

24. Ehnes, Jack, The National Association of Insurance Commissioners, 1995 Workers' Compensation Yearbook, "A Progress Report on the Implementation of 24-Hour Coverage", 1995, p. 56.

25. Gilbert Ecklund, "Oregon to Launch 24-Hour Coverage Pilot Program", Nat'l Underwriter Property & Casualty/Risk and Benefit Management, 10/18/93, p. 27.

26. Tweed, V., "Moving Toward 24-Hour Care", Business and Health, Sept. 1994, p. 54.

27. Annotation Judicial Review of Denial of Health Care Benefits Under Employee Benefit Plan Governed by Employee Retirement Income Security Act (ERISA) 29USCS@1132(a)(1)(B) Post-Firestone cases. Michael A. de Freitas, J.D., adopted from 128 A.L.R. Fed. 1.

28. Minn. R. 5221.6000 - 6500.

29. 537 N.W.2d 480, 487 (Minn. 1995).

30. Research conducted by Professor Richard Butler, University of Minnesota, Carlson School of Management, 1996.

31. David Appel, Philip S. Bora, Richard Doyle, Susan Pantel, Bruce Pyenson, "Workers' Compensation and Health Insurance Reform: An Actuarial and Economic Analysis of Two Proposals", Milliman & Robertson, Inc., 9/14/95.

32. Burton, John F., Jr., Timothy P. Schmidle, 1995 Workers' Compensation Yearbook, LRP Publications, Horsham, PA, 1994, p. 1-45-1-63.

33. Adopted from "Lawyer Urges Close Employer Look at ADA Risks", David M. Katz, Nat'l Underwriter, May 13, 1996.

CHAPTER 15

PENSION PLAN LIABILITY

After Wilson & Brown had been in business for eight years, several of their original employees raised the subject of retirement plans. John and Ann realized that pension plans were essential to keep these skilled employees from looking for another employer.

Employees rate retirement plans as the second most important employee benefit after health insurance.[1] Moreover, retirement plans are probably the most complicated benefit -- in terms of design, administration, taxation and legal obligations.

This chapter covers claims, legal standards and parties of single employer and multiple employer, pension plans under state law, and applies state contract and trust principles to breach of contract claims by plan participants or beneficiaries. Although these principles apply to all types of employee benefit plans, nearly half of all benefit spending by employers is for retirement benefits.

Section 15.1: General Principles

State common law of contract and trust law apply to the following employee benefit and retirement plans, which are exempt from the fiduciary, reporting, and disclosure requirements of ERISA:

1. Governmental plans.

2. Church plans, unless they affirmatively elect to be covered under ERISA.

3. Plans maintained solely to provide only those benefits required by workers' compensation, unemployment compensation or disability insurance laws. (Plans which include other state-mandated benefits are not exempt from ERISA.)[2]

The following plans have been declared by the Secretary of Labor not to be employee welfare benefit plans and are thus exempt from the regulations of ERISA:

1. Compensation for work performed under other than normal circumstances, including over time pay and shift, holiday or week end premiums.

2. Compensation for absences from work due to illness, vacation, holidays, military duty, jury duty or sabbatical leave and training programs to the extent such compensation is paid out of the general assets of the employer.

3. Group insurance programs under which (1) no contributions are made by the employer; (2) participation is completely voluntary for employees; (3) the sole function served by the employer, without endorsing the program, is to

collect premiums through payroll deductions and remit the amount collected to the insurer; and (4) no consideration is paid to the employer in excess of reasonable compensation for administration services actually performed. This includes most mass-marketed insurance plans.

Both ERISA and ERISA-exempt plans are generally IRC tax-qualified or IRC 403(b) plans of educational or governmental units and churches. In this chapter, ERISA is referenced as a standard for these ERISA-exempt plans, since ERISA represents a codification of state trust law, and benefit plan documents commonly incorporate ERISA standards.

For many of these non-ERISA plans there is virtually no state or federal regulation beyond the Internal Revenue Code requirements for qualification and 403 (b) plans, and accountability is to stakeholders or the discipline of market forces is lacking. Without recourse to a regulatory agency or influential parties, a claimant's final resort is a lawsuit for breach of fiduciary duty brought by participants.[3]

ERISA fiduciary standards are used in many non-ERISA areas. A 1981 IRS letter ruling, for example, used the language of ERISA Section 404(a)(1)(B) as a test for determining whether an investment was made for the exclusive benefit of employees, as required under IRC Sec. 404(a).[4] As a practical matter, the ERISA standards have become a national norm for non-ERISA plans.

There is a broad range of ERISA and non-ERISA employee benefit plans. For the purposes of this chapter we assume the ERISA definition of a welfare benefit plan (referenced in Chapter 14 on Employee Health Benefits) applies to the non-ERISA plans here described as any plan, fund or benefit established or maintained by an employer or employee organization to provide participants and beneficiaries through the purchase of insurance or otherwise with any of the following:

- Medical, surgical or hospital care or benefits.
- Benefits in cases of sickness, accident, disability, death or unemployment.
- Vacation benefits.
- Apprenticeship or other training programs.
- Day-care centers.
- Scholarship funds.
- Pre-paid legal services.
- Any benefit described in §302(c) of the Labor Management Relations Act of 1947, such as holiday pay and severance pay.
- Retirement plans.

Section 15.2: Multiple-Employer Benefit Plans

Multiple-Employer Trusts ("METs") are created to fund benefits for employees, often referred to as Multiple-Employer Welfare Arrangements ("MEWAs"). METs are legal entities in the form of trusts (1) sponsored by a person or organization such as a union, a church, a professional organization, an insurance company, an insurance agent/broker or an independent administrator and (2) organized for the purpose of providing group insurance or pension benefits to participants. Each trust must have an administrator and a trustee. The administrator may be a person, organization or an insurance company. A trustee or custodian may be an individual but is usually a corporate trustee such as a commercial bank. METs generally provide group benefits through sponsoring employers within a specific industry such as agriculture, banking, construction, churches, government agencies, or professions.

The benefits provided by each MET may be (1) fully insured and administered by an insurance company, (2) insured but administered by a non insurance company, or (3) not insured and administered by a non insurance company (third party administrator).

A group of employers can participate in a single qualified pension plan, such as a "retirement income account" within the meaning of IRC 403(b)(9), as well as other employee benefit plans offered by the MET. Some plans are collectively bargained plans established under collective bargaining agreements in which the plan is designed and maintained by a labor union and employers who recognize the union contribute to the plan on a basis specified in the collective bargaining agreement. If more than one employer is required to contribute under a single collectively bargained plan, it is known as a multi-employer plan.[5] Plans not arising from a collective bargaining agreement are referred to as multiple-employer plans.

Section 15.3: Parties To The Benefit Contract

Section 15.3(a): Plan Sponsor

The plan sponsor is the party that establishes or maintains the single employer plan or MET. The plan sponsor may be an employee organization, association, committee, joint board of trustees, or other similar group of representatives of the parties involved.

Section 15.3(b): Plan Administrator

The plan administrator is the party contracted to administer plan benefits. In a single employer plan, the employer could be the administrator. Under a MET plan, the administrator is typically a third party engaged in the business of plan administration. This involves communicating benefits to employee/members and processing benefit payments. The administrator is responsible for many clerical and managerial functions related to the plan including record-keeping, receipt and disbursement of funds, claim administration and investments.

A well drafted plan document imposes administrative duties on specific individuals or organizations, thereby attempting to limit the scope of liability to a known group, otherwise persons involved with the plan may be held responsible for actions over which they may think they have no control. This is an important problem in the area of investment decisions. It is therefore important to be as specific as possible in the plan and trust documents as to who has responsibility for making investment decisions and how these persons are chosen. An employee benefit plan subject to ERISA is required to name a plan administrator.

Section 15.3(c): Plan Members or Participants

The plan members are those employees who are plan participants and beneficiaries. As eligible employees, they have elected to participate to receive plan benefits, and their beneficiaries may be eligible to receive plan benefits.

Section 15.3(d): The Benefit Trust

The trust is the leading funding agency for qualified plans, in terms of both number of employees covered and plan assets.[6]

A benefit trust may be formed as a "retirement income account" plan, described in IRC 403(b)(9), and is designed to be exempt from tax under IRC 501(c)(3). The employer organizations which sponsor eligible employees for plan benefits and make contributions on behalf of plan members may also be organizations described in IRC 501(c)(3). The assets of a qualified plan must be held either by a trustee or by an insurance company.

The parties to the plan agreement include: the plan members/employees/beneficiaries, the plan administrator, the plan trust and trustee(s), the plan sponsor, and the sponsoring employers.

Section 15.4: Benefit Plan Fiduciaries

A funded employee benefit plan involves a fiduciary relationship between one who holds and administers plan assets held by a trustee or insurance company, on behalf of plan participants. The definition of a fiduciary is broad enough to include the employer, the plan sponsor, the plan administrator and the trustees; it includes a wide variety of persons. Every plan document must specify a **named fiduciary** in the plan document, providing participants with the parties to name, in case they decide to take legal action. Of course, other named fiduciaries can be included in the legal action.

Five duties of fiduciaries, which are commonly recited in the benefit trust and benefit plan documents and state trust law, are also reflected in ERISA Sec. 404:

1. Solely in the interest of the participants

    "The trustee is under a duty to administer the trust solely in the interest of the beneficiaries."[7]

2. Exclusive purpose of providing benefits to participants

    Most courts have treated the "solely in the interest" and "exclusive purpose" standards interchangeably as codifications of the trust law duty of undivided loyalty.[8]

3. Prudent man rule

    "A trustee shall exercise the care, skill and judgment under the circumstances then prevailing, that a person of ordinary prudence would exercise in the management of their own property and shall consider the role that the investment plays within the trust's overall portfolio of assets."[9]

4. Diversify investments

> "(b) In making and implementing investment decisions, the trustee has a duty to diversify the investments of the trust unless, under the circumstances, it is prudent not do so."[10]

5. Follow documents and instruments of the plan

> "Shall not be compelled to dispose of property. Unless the trust instrument or a court order specifically directs otherwise, a trustee shall not be required to dispose of any property, . . . until the trustee shall determine in exercise of a sound discretion, that it is advisable to dispose of the same, . . ."[11]

"Borrowing from trust law, ERISA imposes higher standards of fiduciary duty upon those responsible for administering an ERISA plan and investing and disposing of its assets. The ERISA fiduciary is subject to a strict standard of care, 29 USC §1104 (a) (1): is liable for known breaches of co-fiduciaries, §1106; and may not engage in prohibited transactions, §1106."[12] ". . . directors of . . . FMC, and company accountants, breached their fiduciary duties under ERISA when they engaged in complex financial transactions . . . thereby wiping out the employees' stock ownership plan . . . We conclude that the Secretary may recover money damages on behalf of the plan for the breaches of duty that did occur."[13]

The trust and plan documents may incorporate ERISA standards such as codifying "the prudent person rule by enacting the so-called 'sole interest' and 'exclusive purpose' rules." 29 U.S.C. Sec.

1104(a)(1) defines the prudent person standard of care: "a fiduciary shall discharge his duties with respect to a plan solely in the interest of the participants and beneficiaries, and -- (A) for the exclusive purpose of providing benefits to participants..and defraying reasonable expenses of administering the plan . . . (B) with the care, skill, prudence, and diligence under the circumstances then prevailing, that a prudent man acting in like capacity and familiar with such matters would use in the conduct of an enterprise of a like character and with like aims; (C) by diversifying the investments of the plan so as to minimize the risk of large losses . . . and (D) in accordance with the documents and instruments governing the plan insofar as such documents and instruments are consistent with the provisions of this subchapter or subchapter III of this chapter."

In addition, the Tax Equity and Fiscal Responsibility Act of 1982 (TEFRA) enacted IRC 403(b)(9), which requires that plan assets "cannot be used for or diverted to purposes other than the exclusive benefit of employees and their beneficiaries."

Section 15.5: Fiduciary Relationships and Contracting Parties

The agreement between plan participants and fiduciaries is a contract which incorporates the stricter standards of fiduciary law. Robert Clark identified some of the distinctive attributes that characterize fiduciary relationships. "Fiduciary law is stricter on fiduciaries than contract law is on ordinary contracting parties, in at least four fundamental respects. There are stricter rules about disclosure, more open-ended duties to act, tighter delineations of rights to compensation and to benefits that could flow from one's position, and more intrusive normative rhetoric."[14] Fiduciaries such as corporate directors, directors of mutual funds, ERISA fiduciaries, and trustees of personal trusts may all be held personally liable for breaches of their duties.[15]

An ERISA trustee or fiduciary is to discharge its fiduciary duties in accordance with the plan and trust documents governing the plan, but only to the extent that those documents conform with the fiduciary provisions of ERISA Sec. 404(a)(1)(A-D), 29 U.S.C. §1104(a)(1)(A-D). ERISA standards do not permit the trust creator or the plan sponsor to dictate policies which exculpate the trustees from their strong fiduciary duties to plan participants. Minnesota trust law and statutes, like ERISA, recognize only economic objectives and does not countenance non-economic considerations at the expense of return or risk.

An IRS General Counsel Memorandum published on April 20, 1992, concludes, "A provision in a trust agreement violates the exclusive benefit rule of Section 401(a)(2) for the purposes of plan qualification, where the trustee is allowed to consider non-financial, employment-related factors in tendering, voting and handling of securities." In addition, the DOL has determined that plan provisions permitting trustees' consideration of employment factors in a tender offer would violate ERISA Sec. 404(a) in its enforcement of the exclusive benefit rule. TRES. REG. SEC.I.401-2(a)(3) explains that the phrase "Purposes other than the exclusive benefit of his employees or their beneficiaries" includes "all objects or aims not solely designated for the proper satisfaction of all liabilities to employees or their beneficiaries covered by the Trust."[16]

A case indicating that plan members may have a cause of action against the plan administrator when erroneous information is given by the administrator is Dahlgren v. U.S. West, Inc., 12 E.B.C. 2275 (D. Ore. 1990). This case started as a malpractice action by an alternate payee against her family law attorney. The case became more interesting when the attorney filed a third-party claim against U.S. West as sponsor of the pension plan for which the attorney had negotiated a Qualified Domestic Relations Order ("QDRO"). The attorney wanted U.S. West to indemnify her for any amounts she might be required to pay her client as a result of the malpractice action. The basis for the attorney's claim against U.S. West was some erroneous information the attorney obtained from the company regarding the amount of benefit payments her client would receive from its pension plan as a result of the QDRO. While it wasn't a decision on the merits of the attorney's claim, the court denied U.S. West's motion for summary judgment after finding that the claim was not preempted by ERISA.

Section 15.6: Contractual Nature of Pension Benefits

It has long been recognized that pension benefits represent compensation in the form of deferred wages, enforceable in an action on a contract. This view of fringe benefits as deferred wages was first recognized in 1949.[17] Therefore, common law contract principles apply to benefits which the plan promises and the participant makes application to participate in.

Common law contract principles where augmented by trust law applicable to many employee retirement plan trusts, even prior to enactment of ERISA. As one court noted, "The law governing the administration of pensions is a hybrid born of a marriage of contract and trust principles. Over the years, both fields of law vied for the dominant role. At first, courts fastened on the contractual nature of pensions . . . Later cases, however, have accorded increasing weight to the fiduciary obligations borne by the trustees for the benefit of the employees."[18]

Generally interpretation of an employee benefit plan must begin with the plan documentation including the official "written instrument and/or the summary plan description."[19] Interpretation of plan benefits begins with a review of Plan Descriptions, Trust Documents, Summary Plan Descriptions and all other written and oral communications between the parties regarding benefit descriptions and promises.

"Pension plans constitute enforceable contracts."[20]

"In reviewing the trustees' decision, it must be remembered that a pension plan is a contract between an employer and its employees."[21]

Under an ERISA plan, an ". . . employee nevertheless may acquire contractual interest in such (welfare benefit) plans benefits, enforceable under federal common law.[22]

"The Court looks to the state common law of contracts as guidance in formulating a sound federal common law rule with which to analyze the rights and obligations of the parties."[23]

"Deferred retirement benefits earned during active employment are enforceable contract rights."[24]

The court is to consider the "spirit and the purpose of the contract, as well as its letter."[25]

Section 15.7: Breach of Contract

A contract is "a promise or a set of promises for the breach of which the law gives a remedy or the performance of which the law recognizes a duty."[26] The contract, in the case of a single or multiple employer benefit plan, is formed in part by the applications of eligible employees and the above listed documents describing the plan benefits under which the plan sponsor, administrator, trustee and employer promised to administer the plan "solely in the interest" of the members and for the "exclusive purpose of providing benefits."

A contract is not formed unless there is an offer, acceptance and consideration.[27] An offer must be definite in form and "is the manifestation of willingness to enter into a bargain, so made as to justify another person in understanding that his assent to the bargain is invited and will conclude it."[28] The offer must be communicated to the offeree.[29]

The offer is typically made to eligible employees by the pension administrator on behalf of the plan sponsor, trustees and the employers.

An acceptance is effective once it is communicated directly to the offeror.[30] Such notification is excused only where the offer itself indicates that notification is unnecessary.[31]

The element of consideration requires a bargained for performance or return promise.[32] "To constitute consideration a benefit or detriment must be 'bargained for'."[33] "Bargaining" in this sense refers to the process of negotiation which results in the assumption of an obligation by one party upon the promise of an act or forbearance by the other.[34]

Section 15.8: Basic Rules of Insurance Contract Interpretation are Applicable

Since the participants' benefit contract is a contract of adhesion, the following principles of contract interpretation, also applicable to insurance contracts, apply to the agreement:

1. As a contract of adhesion, any ambiguities or inconsistencies are interpreted in favor of the participants and beneficiaries. "Employer's pension and death benefit plan for employees must be read as a whole and ambiguities resolved against employer."[35]

2. The reasonable expectation of participants and beneficiaries should be honored if contract language is objectively contrary to those reasonable expectations. To discern the objective intent of the parties to an employee benefit plan, emphasis should be placed on the reasonable expectations of the beneficiaries, as ERISA was designed to protect their interests.[36]

One "reasonable expectation" of plan members is that the administrator will provide benefits and administer the plan "solely" in their interest and for the "exclusive purpose" of providing benefits.

3. Grants of benefits in contract language are broadly applied and restrictions or limitations are narrowly construed.

4. The doctrines of concealment and misrepresentation are applicable, as they would be to insurance contracts, in the same fashion that employee medical benefits contracts are subject to the same standards.

5. The benefits agreement, or insurance policy, should be read as a whole and words shall be given their ordinary meaning.

Section 15.9: The Benefit Agreement

The benefit agreement consists of the promises made by the parties and the benefit provisions of the following documents:

1. Membership application completed by an eligible employee.
2. Documents provided by the plan administrator to eligible employees as part of the enrollment process:

    (i) Invitations to information meetings;
    (ii) A summary plan description (SPD);
    (iii) A sample individual benefit statement;
    (iv) A brief summary of plan benefits;

(v)	A booklet on plan-investment choices;
(vi)	An application form; and
(vii)	Information on plan contributions.

3. The following plan documents are the ultimate contract reference for benefit language:

(i)	The master benefit/pension plan document.
(ii)	The benefit/pension trust document.

Allegations of breach of contract and breach of fiduciary duty are commonly made by plan members and beneficiaries. A combination of contract and trust law is applicable in these cases.

Every qualified plan must include a written procedure under which a claimant can appeal denial of a plan benefit to the plan administrator. This assumes the claim is not satisfactorily resolved internally, and claimants exercise their right to sue, claiming that the plan administrator, trustees, plan sponsor and employers breached the benefits agreement and their fiduciary duties, and seek a remedy such as rescission of the contract and return of the benefit funds.

Section 15.10: Claims and Litigation[37]

A number of claims are likely to be asserted by plan participants and beneficiaries, when plan investments do not perform as expected. The claims will generally cover one or more of the following categories:

Section 15.10(a): Fiduciary Imprudence

1. Claimants allege that the fiduciary selecting the investment failed to act solely in the best interests of plan participants and beneficiaries as, for example, required by ERISA Sec. 404 when it

   a. failed to fully evaluate the financial strength and stability of the issuer,
   b. failed to adequately consider alternatives to this issuer or this investment,
   c. failed to communicate and to take timely action when an investment began to show signs of failure or financial difficulty.

2. Claimants allege that the fiduciary failed to properly diversify the portfolio by purchasing other investments or from other issuers, for example, violating ERISA Sec. 404(a)(1)(c).

3. Claimants allege that a trustee who held the investment after its purchase was directed by a named fiduciary who failed to accept "proper direction" by completing the transaction, and should have acted either to

   a. not complete the transaction after independent analysis at the outset; or
   b. reconsidered the investment in this asset at some time after the purchase, once

negative financial information and ratings were made public.

4. Claimants allege that certain non-fiduciaries were knowing participants in the transaction; they are therefore subject to the same penalties for fiduciary breach imposed on fiduciaries and co-fiduciaries under ERISA Sec. 404, 405 and 502(1).

Section 15.10(b): Prohibited Transactions of both IRC Section 4975 and ERISA Section 406

A prohibited transaction is a "**transfer to**", or the "**use by**" or "**for the benefit of**" a party-in-interest, of any assets of the plan.

The plan sponsor may be a party-in-interest, and its investment directions may be "for the benefit of" the sponsor. Although this may be stretching to a degree the prohibited transactions listed in ERISA, it shows the types of transactions which are prohibited and transactions which violate the spirit of ERISA when investments directed by and influenced by the interests of an outside organization. An employer or employee organization is an outside organization and is a party-in-interest. Certainly the direction of voting the proxies and shareholder development by a plan sponsor, for example, violates the spirit, at least, of the prohibited transaction section of ERISA.

Consideration of the non-financial factors violates the exclusive benefit rule of IRC 401(a)(2) for the purposes of plan qualification where the trustee is allowed to consider non-financial factors in the tendering, voting and handling of securities.[38]

Section 15.10(c): Defective or Misleading Communications

A "claimant may allege that the issuer misrepresented the true nature of the investments, thereby misleading participants into thinking that the investment was "safer" than it really was. This claim may be asserted either against the issuer by participants or fiduciaries, or by participants against the fiduciary which chose the investment for the plan. For example:

1. Claimants allege that employee communications misstated:

    (a) the safety of the fund;
    (b) the nature of the assets in the fund;
    (c) the lack of diversity in the fund.

2. Claimants allege that the plan sponsor failed to provide:

    (a) adequate financial information from which participants could evaluate their plan's investment options;
    (b) information concerning changes in financial stability or ratings of issuers of assets held in the funds.

Section 15.10(d): Failure to Comply with Plan Provisions

A claimant may allege that the plan administrators failed to operate the plans in accordance with plan provisions, violating, for example, ERISA Sec. 404(a)(1)(D) by:

(a) causing payouts from plan assets other than through the payout provisions of the insurance contracts;

(b) improperly investing the plan according to plan provisions and restrictions.

Section 15.10(e): Impermissible Reduction in Benefits

In cases where benefits are paid from insurance contracts and those benefit payments are reduced or suspended, plaintiffs allege that the plan sponsor has impermissibly reduced benefits under the plan provisions, in violation of, for example, ERISA Sec. 203. The ERISA section on limitation of liability of plan fiduciaries indicate what instructions or actions plan fiduciaries may or may not be liable for any loss.

Section 15.10(f): Effect of Compliance - Limitation on Liability of Plan Fiduciaries - Sec. 2550.404c-1(d)(2)

A fiduciary is not liable for any loss, or any breach under Part 4 of Title I of ERISA ("Fiduciary Responsibility"), that is the result of participant's exercise of control, except for instructions which:

(h) Are not in accordance with the plan documents.
(i) Would cause a fiduciary to maintain indicia of ownership of assets outside the jurisdiction of U.S. district courts (unless otherwise permitted by Section 404(b) of ERISA).
(j) Would jeopardize the plan's tax qualified status.
(k) Could result in loss greater than the participant's account balance.
(l) Would result in the direct sale, exchange, lease or other prohibited transaction involving property between the plan sponsor and the plan.

A fiduciary is still responsible for initial selection and periodic review of investment alternatives made available to participants.

Section 15.10(g): Social Investing

The question of whether there is a role in pension investing for active attempts to support a particular social result, not guided by market conditions, has been addressed in journal articles and court cases. However, existing statutes related to qualified plan investments focus primarily on fiduciary duties in the relationship between plan managers and participants, and do not directly address investments to support a social result. These statutes and supporting common law encourage investment managers to prevent direct losses to participants and beneficiaries and to avoid risk, particularly of large losses through, for example, a requirement for diversification, but do not directly deal with possible indirect losses as a result of socially-directed investments which may impact the economic interests of plan participants. The plan directive for investment plan managers is to prudently balance risk and return on economic market bases within limits dictated by ERISA-type fiduciary standards.

The goals of social investing fall into two classifications: (1) to support the direct economic interests of plan participants, (2) to support moral or political interests of a broader group of plan participants. The first classification includes the following: (1) curtailing investment policies which contribute to disinvestment in basic industries or certain geographical areas which may result in loss of jobs for participants covered under the pension plan; (2) encouraging investment in housing and other facilities in communities where plan participants live; (3) curtailing investment in non-unionized corporations which might undermine the union movement where plan participants are union members; (4) avoiding investments in corporations that violate health, safety or non-discrimination principles which impact on the interests of plan participants; (5) attempts to prohibit overseas investments and investments in energy resources directly competing with coal.

In Cowan v. Scargill (1985) 1Ch 270, an English case, the Chancery Division held that the trustees of a miners workers union pension plan acted in violation of their fiduciary duties when they attempted to prohibit overseas investment in energy sources directly competing with coal. The court ruled that trustees power must be exercised so as to yield the best return for beneficiaries, judged in relation to risks of the investments in question.[39]

Social investment objectives which fall under the second classification relating to moral or political grounds include investments relating to (1) environmental pollution, (2) companies doing business in South Africa under the apartheid system, (3) weapons production, (4) race discrimination, (5) fair employment and (6) consumer responsibility. These are not directly related to the economic interests of plan participants and are therefore void.

15.10(h): Employers Now Can Offer 401(k) Advice

While employers cannot make specific investment recommendations to employees, they can come close, according to new June 1996 Department of Labor rules. Without fear of liability, employers now can provide to employees:

- basic financial and investment information
- suggestions for dividing money among stock and bond mutual funds, depending on age and risk tolerance
- worksheets or computer software to let employees calculate potential returns for different mixes of mutual funds

The rules were prompted by the explosive growth of 401(k) plans. About 23 million people have $740 billion in the plans. The average balance is $32,000 today versus $10,500 in 1985 (source: Access Research). There is a growing group of consultants providing financial planning tailored to 401(k) participants.

Section 15.10(i): Rescission Remedy

A material breach of a contract or a substantial failure in its performance justifies an aggrieved party in rescinding it.[40]

Moreover, the equitable remedy of rescission of a contract is available when the breach of an essential part of the contract is irreparable or when the damages would be difficult or impossible to determine or would be inadequate.[41]

In addition, traditional trust law provides for broad and flexible equitable remedies in cases involving breaches of fiduciary duty. Trust law provides the remedy of restoring plan participants to the position in which they would have occupied but for the breach of trust.[42]

Under ERISA, 29 U.S.C. §1109: "Any person who is a fiduciary with respect to a plan who breaches any of the responsibilities, obligations, or duties imposed upon fiduciaries . . . shall be subject to such other equitable or remedial relief that the court may deem appropriate . . ."

The legislative reports of the various committees of Congress, in drafting ERISA, make it clear that Congress intended to provide the courts with broad remedies for redressing the interests of participants and beneficiaries when they have been adversely affected by breaches of fiduciary duty.[43]

Rescission is granted only where a material breach or substantial failure in the performance of the contract has occurred.[44]

A "material" breach must go to the whole consideration "such as to defeat the purpose of the contract."[45] Rescission is a drastic remedy, the "unmaking of a contract," which "not only terminates the contract but abrogates it and undoes it from the beginning."[46]

Where a party has already substantially performed its part of an agreement and cannot be returned to the status quo, the other party may not rescind the agreement but must instead bring an action for damages.[47] As the Minnesota Supreme Court has explained:

> One wishing to rescind the contract for breach thereof must act promptly. After one party to a contract has performed a substantial part of it, the other party cannot rescind for default in further performance unless the defaulting party can be placed in status quo, but is limited to an action for damages for the breach. It is not every breach of contract which justifies rescission. The right to rescind must therefore be exercised promptly on discovery of the facts from which it arises and it is clear under the law that it may be waived by continuing to treat the contract as a subsisting obligation.[48]

Moreover, when ordering rescission would be too disruptive, causing more harm than it would remedy, the court should deny a request for the drastic remedy of rescission.[49] Because restitution is an equitable remedy, general equitable considerations apply in determining whether it should be granted.[50]

15.11: Summary

Employers' legal responsibilities are framed under ERISA and non-ERISA pension plans. However, state law also applies to non-ERISA pension plans, to state workers' compensation benefits and to health insurance contracts, as reviewed in Chapter 14.

1. Employee Benefit Research Institute, Issue Brief No. 111, Washington, D.C. (2/91).

2. Adopted from Employee Benefits, Beam & McFadden, Dearborn Pub. 1994.

3. See Withers v. Teachers Retirement System of the City of New York, 447 F. Supp. 1248 (S.D. N.Y. 1978), aff'd 595 F.2d 1210 (2nd Cir. 1979) and in Donovan v. Bierwirth, 680 F.2d 263 (2nd Cir. 1982).

4. IRS letter ruling on bond purchases by Detroit Public Plans, (BNA) No. 371, J-9 (Dec. 7, 1981).

5. IRS Code §404(f).

6. Beam & McFadden, at 421.

7. Am.L.I. Restatement, Law of Trusts, 3rd Sec. 170, "Duty of Loyalty".

8. Donovan, 680 F.2d at 271, and Eaves v. Penn, 587 F.2d 453, 457 (10th Cir. 1978).

9. Minn. Stat. §501B.10.

10. Am.L.I. Restatement Law of Trusts, 3rd, Sec. 227.

11. Section 501B.10 Subd. 2.

12. Martin v. Feilen, 965 F.2d 660, 664: 1992 US App., 15 E.B.C. 1545.

13. Id. at 660.

14. Robert Clark, Agency Costs versus Fiduciary Duties, Principals and Agents: The Structure of the Business, 55, 76 (1985).

15. Krikorian, Fiduciary Standards in Pension & Trust Fund Management, p. 9-3 (Butterworth: 2nd ed. 1994).

16. Gen. Counsel Mem. 38970.

17. Inland Steel Co. v. NLRB, 170 F.2d 272 (7th Cir. 1948), cert. denied, 336 U.S. 960 (1949).

18. Valle v. Joint Plumbing Indus., 623 F.2d 196, 207, 3 EBC 1026, 1035 (2nd Cir. 1980), quoting Mitzner v. Jarcho, 44 N.Y.2d 39 (1978).

19. See, e.g. Musto v. American General Corp., 861 F.2d 897, 900-01 (6th Cir. 1988); 29 U.S.C. §1022, §1102(a)(1).

20. Sedman v. Michigan Bell Telephone Co., 336 N.W.2d 868 (Mich. Ct. App. 1983), citing Psutka v. Michigan Alkali Co., 274 Mich. 318, 264 N.W. 385 (1936); Couch v. Administrative Committee of the Difco Laboratories, Inc., Salaried Employees Profit Sharing Trust, 44 Mich. App. 44, 205 N.W.2d (1972).

21. Audio Fidelity v. Pension Guaranty Corp., 624 F.2d 513 (4th Cir. 1980); Monsanto Co. v. Ford, 534 F. Supp. 51 (D.C.Mo. 1981); see also Childs v. National Bank of Austin, 658 F.2d 487 (7th Cir. 1981).

22. Employee Retirement Income Security Act of 1974, ss 201-306, as amended, 29 U.S.C.A. §§ 1051-1086." Musto v. American General Corp., 615 F.Supp. 1483 (D.C. Tenn. 1985).

23. In re White Farm Equipment Co., 42 B.R. 1005 (Bankr.N.D. Ohio 1984), expedited appeal granted (April 15, 1985), suggestion of bankruptcy filed staying appeal (June 24, 1985).

24. Hoefel v. Atlas Tack Corp., 581 F.2d 1, 4 (1st Cir. 1978), cert. denied, 440 U.S. 913, 99 S.Ct. 1227, 59 L.Ed. 2d 462 (1979).

25. Clap v. Hofferman Water Conditioning Inc., 380 N.W.2d 838, 841 (Minn. Ct. App. 1986), (quoting Marso v. Mankato Clinic, Ltd., 286 Minn. 104, 153 N.W.2d 281 (1967)).

26. Baehr v. Penn-O-Tex Oil Corp., 104 N.W.2d 661, 664-5 (Minn. 1960).

27. Cederstrand v. Lutheran Brotherhood, 117 N.W.2d 213, 219-21 (Minn. 1962).

28. Restatement (Second) of Contracts §24 (1979); Pine River State Bank v. Mettille, 333 N.W.2d 622, 626 (Minn. 1983).

29. Pine River, 333 N.W.2d at 626.

30. 451 Corp. v. Pension System for Policemen and Firemen of Detroit, 310 N.W.2d 922, 924 (Minn. 1981).

31. Restatement (Second) of Contracts §56 (1979).

32. Restatement (Second) of Contracts §71 (1979).

33. Minnesota JIG 626 (3rd edition), Authorities at 425.

34. Baehr, supra.

35. Psutka v. Michigan Alkali Co., 264 N.W. 385, 386 (1936).

36. Sprague v. General Motors, 843 F.Supp. 266, 307 (E.D. Mich. 1994).

37. Much of the material in this section was adapted from "investment Guidelines for ERISA Investments", by Lucinda Hruska-Clarys, pp. 8-11, M.I.L.E. Employee Benefits, 1994.

38. General Counsel Memorandum 39870, January 23, 1992.

39. This case cited two American cases: Blankenship v. Boyle, 229 F.Supp. 1089 (D.D.C. 1971) and Withers v. Teachers Retirement System of the City of New York, 447 F.Supp. 1248 (S.D. N.Y. 1978), aff'd 595 F.2d 1210 (2nd Cir. 1979).

40. Distronics Corp. v. Roberts-Hamiltion Co., 575 F. Supp. 275 (D. Minn. 1983); Village of Wells v. Layne-Minnesota Co., 60 N.W.2d 621 (Minn. 1953).

41. Marso, 153 N.W.2d at 278.

42. Restatement of Trusts (Second) §205, comment a.

43. <u>Eaves v. Penn</u>, 587 F.2d 453, 462 (10th Cir. 1978) (citing S. Rep. No. 93-127, 93d Cong., 1st Sess., Reprinted [1974] U.S. Code Cong. & Admin. News, pp. 4838, 4871).

44. <u>Heyn v. Braun</u>, 59 N.W.2d 326, 330 (Minn. 1953).

45. <u>United Cigar Stores Co. v. Hollister</u>, 242 N.W. 3, 4 (Minn. 1932).

46. <u>Johnny's, Inc. v. Njaka</u>, 450 N.W.2d 166, 168 (Minn. Ct. App. 1990).

47. <u>Heyn v. Braun</u>, 59 N.W.2d at 330. See also <u>Northern Pac. Ry. Co. v. United States</u>, 70 F. Supp. 836, 865 (D. Minn. 1946), aff'd 188 F.2d 277 (8th Cir. 1951).

48. <u>Cut Price Super Markets v. Kingpin Foods</u>, 98 N.W.2d 257, 267 (Minn. 1959).

49. 2 Dobbs, <u>Law of Remedies</u> §9.3(2), at 582 n. 8. See also <u>Village of Wells, supra</u> (rescission denied where restitution was impossible due to no fault of defendant); <u>Stronge Warner Co. v. H. Choate & Co.</u>, 182 N.W. 712 (Minn. 1921) (where restoration to prior positions is impractical, even where material breaches are found, only damages, if any, are available); <u>Carlson v. Segog</u>, 62 N.W. 1132 (Minn. 1895) (rescission denied because parties could not be placed in <u>status quo ante</u>).

50. 2 Dobbs, <u>Law of Remedies</u>, §9.6 at 624.

CHAPTER 16

RISK MANAGEMENT

After 15 years in business, Wilson & Brown had been sued for discrimination, products liability, breach of contract, and for a customer's "slip and fall" injuries on an icy sidewalk. John and Ann talked to their business friends, and realized theirs was a typical experience. Such lawsuits against businesses are now routine, and are a significant economic drain. John and Ann decided to retain a risk management consultant to reduce the risk and expense of litigation.

Risk management involves the administration of a carefully-developed process to efficiently protect income, assets, and human resources. Effective risk management is based on two underlying principles: (1) Murphy's Law, with a vengeance -- if the worst can happen, it will, at the worst possible time, and if it has just happened, it will soon occur again; and (2) the Scout's motto, "Be Prepared". Risk management prepares business for the worst possible losses.

The steps to maintaining the risk management process seem obvious and simple: (1) risk identification, (2) risk measurement, (3) selecting risk-control methods, (4) selecting risk-financing methods including insurance, and (5) administering and monitoring RM program.

16.1: Risk Identification

"Forewarned is Forearmed!" This first, and most important step involves discovery of all loss exposures to people, cash flow and assets. People are the most critical business asset. This chapter focuses primarily on management of liability (including workers' compensation) and property exposures. (Risk management of medical expenses, income loss and retirement programs is beyond the scope of this book.)

Your business must systematically identify risks to determine which risk control and risk financing techniques to apply. The following tools are normally employed:

1. **Loss Exposure Checklists.** Select loss exposures applicable to your business. Three commonly cited risk analysis questionnaires are published by the American Management Association (AMA)[1], the Risk Management Insurance Management Society (RIMS), and the International Risk Management Institute (IRMI). Some other questionnaires have been designed for specific industries, such as AMA's Risk Analysis Guide to Insurance and Employee Benefits.[2] Such checklists are useful starting points for the development of an overall exposure review. However, standard checklists fail to list risks that are unusual or unique to a particular business, so the following additional exposure review methods should be applied.

2. **Insurance Policy Checklists.** Review insurance policy checklists used to identify insurance applicable to your firm such as McCormick's <u>Coverages Applicable</u>, listing applicable insurance policies for many types of businesses. Many of these coverages will be included in a package policy, such as a commercial package policy or a business owners policy. Personal policies, such as personal auto policies and homeowners policies, must be integrated with the business coverages.

3. **Financial Statements Review.** Financial statements, balance sheet, profit/loss or operating statements, budgets and process flow charts to identify important assets, cash flows, and critical business processes should be reviewed. Each account title is reviewed in depth to assess its potential risks. How do cash amounts vary over time? Where is cash located? Who has access? What control systems are in place?

For accounts receivable, what and where are records kept? Are duplicates and back up records stored off premises? What amounts are likely to be uncollected if records are destroyed? A word of caution--do not rely on the dollar amounts shown on the balance sheet for RM decisions. Business interruption insurance can be purchased to cover net profit and continuing expense losses.

4. **Other Risk Identification Methods.**

(1) Review organizational structure, key personnel, and decision procedures.

(2) Inspection of property and operations.

Risk Management

(3) Review contracts, leases, purchase agreements, and agreements with independent contractors.

(4) Review past loss experience.

5. **Commonly Unrecognized Exposures.** Application of these methods may result in identification of the following previously unrecognized loss exposures:

(1) Business interruption and loss of cash flow after damage to business assets, or damage to a critical supplier's plant, or to a large customer's premises. Ask your insurance agent or broker for review of business interruption and contingent business interruption coverages. Businesses with full insurance on buildings and equipment have failed to reopen after fire losses because of no insurance on loss of net profit and expenses which continue after the fire.

(2) Employee benefit plan liability. Review coverage both for benefit administration and fiduciary liability.

(3) Loss of valuable papers, accounts receivable records, documents, data, or client files. Frequent file duplication on off-premises storage is often advised.

(4) Non-owned auto or non-owned watercraft liability. Personal auto liability insurance covers

many business uses; business insurance should be coordinated with personal insurance. For example, non-owned auto liability insurance will cover limits in excess of the owner's personal auto insurance.

(5) Contractual liability assumed under leases, purchase orders, service agreements, etc. Some personal liability policies cover oral contracts. Business contractual coverage must be specifically purchased.

(6) Liability for acts of independent contractors. Yes, you can be sued for the acts of independent contractors and you may have a contractual obligation to indemnify independent contractors.

(7) Liability for discrimination or harassment. General liability insurance excludes this, but special coverage is available.

16.2: Risk Measurement

The second step in the risk management process involves evaluating the impact of the identified loss exposures and planning for future possible losses. The potential severity, frequency, and risk of the identified exposures is assessed and related to the business's financial capacity, as a basis for deciding which exposures to insure and the type and amount of insurance to purchase. The business must specify the cash flow it can afford to lose in a budget period, as a beginning basis for assessing self-insurance and deductible levels. This information, combined with the business's risk aversion attitude and goals, is used to design an effective and efficient risk-management framework with which to approach insurance carriers. Risks should be ranked in order of priority by severity or magnitude, and by whether insurance is required by law or contract. Appraisal of property values, assessing liability limits, and measurement of cash flows is necessary for designing a risk management program and designing the insurance program.

16.3: Methods of Risk Control

To prevent and reduce losses, management develops the best combination of risk control methods.

16.3(a): Loss Prevention

This involves removing or controlling hazards that make losses more likely to occur. Prevention activities include lumbar support belts, training and exercises for proper lifting of heavy crates, product safety features, warning labels, and customer education to reduce the number of injury and product liability claims. Systematic documentation of decision-making also reduces the number of lawsuits.

Do not provide services to high-hazard clients/customers, and make appropriate referrals when requested services are beyond your competent delivery capabilities. Avoid the high risk property, person, or activity by refusing to engage it or by abandoning a loss exposure.

Don't sell a service or stop producing a product or service due to high risk.

16.3(b): Loss Reduction

Loss reduction programs limit the size of losses. A sprinkler system is a classic example, because fire must occur before the system reduces the damage. Loss reduction involves post-loss activities planned prior to the loss. Salvage measures and subrogation in insurance reduce loss due to payment from third parties. Arbitration, mediation, and public relations efforts are post-loss reduction strategies. Catastrophe or contingency plans are a coordinated approach to loss reduction. Maintaining inventories, spare parts, duplicate machinery, or temporary human resources can reduce post-loss cost. Separating exposure units can reduce the chance of catastrophic loss. Small business management requires consulting assistance in all these areas.

16.3(c): Insurance Company Safety Services

Insurers typically provide safety and loss prevention advice to insureds. Additionally, some states require insurers to annually notify insureds of their right to safety and occupational laws consultation services, and upon written request, to provide occupational health, loss control and safety consultation services including work place surveys to identify safety problems, review of employer injury records, and development of plans to improve health and safety. In Minnesota, employers and self-insureds may obtain loans from the Assigned Risk Safety Account if the employer has had an on-site safety survey conducted by specified inspectors or consultants, including an in-house employee safety and health committee, and the on-sight safety survey recommends specific safety practices for equipment to reduce injuries.[3]

16.3(d): Worker's Compensation Reporting and Penalties

Because an increasing amount of vital information is expected from employers, the business may need help from a broker or consultant to comply with all state-mandated worker's compensation reporting requirements.

For example, most states assess penalties against businesses that fail to post a notice advising employees of specific worker's compensation rights and obligations. An employer's failure to carry worker's compensation insurance or comply with the state's self-insurance program can result in penalties of $10,000 or more. An employer that enters into an unlawful agreement whereby employees pay part of the employer's worker's compensation costs may pay a penalty of 400% or more of the amount withheld from the employee.

Also, some states require a report providing data on the promptness of worker's compensation payments. This data will be available to employers to assist them in selecting insurers and in monitoring claim payment services.

16.4: Selecting Insurance to Purchase

Business insurance coverages are discussed generally in Chapter 11. This section provides an example of how to select liability/property insurance. Coverages are listed by priority in three categories: essential, advisable, and available coverages.

16.4(a): Essential Coverages

Essential coverages are those required by law, under contract, or to cover catastrophic losses. For most businesses, they include the following:

1. **Workers' Compensation Insurance.** Firms with employees are required by state law to purchase workers' comp insurance or have approved self insurance. The worker's compensation policy pays benefits specified by each state's statutes and covers the employee's liability for work connected employee injury. Beyond the workers' compensation laws (WCL), employers' liability remains for (1) employees not covered by WCL, (2) employees disabled by a job-related disease not covered by WCL, (3) employees may assume liability for claims against fellow employees, (4) liability for spouses of injured employees, insured employees who sue in a "dual capacity" not as an employee, but as a customer or patient, and (5) employers who elected out of WCL. In a few states, such as Texas, an employer can elect to "opt out" of the workers' compensation statutes.

2. **Auto liability insurance**, with inadequate limits, is required by the statutes in most states and poses a catastrophic loss potential. A business auto policy should cover ownership, maintenance, and use of any automobile, including owned car, hired car, and non-ownership liability. Umbrella/excess liability limits should be purchased with a high maximum because of the unlimited loss potential. Umbrella/excess policies also provide the critically important legal defense services

which are provided by the underlying liability insurer until policy limits are paid.

3. **General liability insurance** covers many catastrophic losses. The commercial general liability ("CGL") policy automatically covers new sources of liability which develop during the policy period. Coverage limits, as with auto and other liability coverages, should be coordinated with high umbrella/excess limits. General liability exposures and coverages are so numerous, complex, and potentially catastrophic that they must be selected working with a consultant, broker or attorney specializing in insurance.

4. **Employee benefit plan liability and fiduciary liability insurance.** Review coverage both for benefit administration and fiduciary liability. Fiduciary liability insurance covers employers obligations under the Federal Employee Retirement Income Security Act ("ERISA") or similar law. ERISA does not require this important liability insurance, but the potential loss to directors and officers as a fiduciary is catastrophic. ERISA does require that every fiduciary be bonded, which only covers loss due to dishonesty. The bond is commonly an inexpensive addition to the CGL policy.

5. **Directors and officers ("D & O") insurance.** Covers the corporate principals when they are named as defendants in a lawsuit based on their corporate work.

6. **Professional liability coverages.** Most businesses offering professional services are subject to potentially catastrophic negligence claims. Policy limits should be high and coordinated with umbrella/excess policy limits, which must be scrutinized since the umbrella/excess policy may exclude professional services.

7. **Non-owned auto or non-owned watercraft liability.** Personal auto liability insurance covers many business

uses; business insurance should be coordinated with personal insurance. For example, non-owned auto liability insurance will cover limits in excess of the owner's personal auto insurance.

8. **Contractual liability** assumed under leases, purchase orders, service agreements, etc. Some personal liability policies cover oral contracts. Business contractual coverage must be specifically purchased.

9. **Liability for acts of independent contractors.** Yes, you can be sued for the acts of independent contractors and you may have a contractual obligation to indemnify independent contractors.

10. **Liability for discrimination or harassment.** General liability insurance excludes this, but special coverage is available.

11. **Employment practices liability Insurance** in hiring, reviewing, promoting or discharging employees, particularly owner/executives. General liability insurance excludes this, but special coverage is available.

12. **Commercial property insurance coverages** for buildings and personal property. Policies should pay on a "replacement cost basis." Mortgagees typically require this insurance and should be named insureds on each policy. A RM consultant or insurance broker can advise about proper policy provisions, including waiver of coinsurance (so the insured does not have to pay a part of a partial loss), buying blanket limits, and covering all causes of physical damage not excluded. Boiler and machinery coverage and earthquake and flood insurance are important coverage additions.

13. **Business interruption insurance.** This covers income loss occurring after damage to covered owned property and is added to the commercial property policy. Contingent

business interruption covers income losses occurring after covered property damage to suppliers or customers property.

14. **Health, life, and pension benefits.** While not required by state or federal law, health and life insurance cover potentially catastrophic losses and some firms must provide these benefits under contract with employees. These policies must be coordinated with the business owner's personal insurance.

15. **Insurance to fund a buy and sell agreement.** A buy and sell agreement typically requires buying and selling of company shares when an owner dies, is disabled or retires. Life and disability insurance is commonly purchased to fund the buy and sell and may be coordinated with key person insurance.

Unemployment compensation and social security benefits are essential coverages required by law and take a total of 16+% of payroll (employees plus employer's share), but do not involve the purchase of private insurance. Some employers and employees can avoid the immediate tax on payroll by engaging independent contractors rather than employees by using health care and dependent care reimbursement accounts, and can minimize unemployment compensation tax by avoiding the necessity of terminating employees. To qualify for unemployment compensation, an employee must have been terminated rather than quit, must have worked a certain length of time prior to termination, must be actively seeking replacement work, and not have been terminated for misconduct.

Commercial litigation is frustrating for both businesses and their liability insurers. First, many lawsuits are unnecessary -- they can be avoided with basic claims-prevention procedures. Second, after the litigation begins, the business and insurer usually realize that the insurance purchased was inadequate to fully cover and service the claim.

Liability and insurance management addresses both of these problems. First, the business employs claims-prevention measures that reduce the number of claims. Second, the business purchases the coverages and claims-management services which match its liability exposures, reducing the likelihood of an uncovered claim. This article provides business and insurance examples addressing both of these "lines of defense".

16.4(b): Advisable Coverages

The following coverages are illustrative of insurance for serious but not catastrophic losses. Without these coverages, losses would be difficult financially but would not result in business termination:

1. Coverage for accounts receivable, valuable papers, or information systems. Typically inland marine coverage for damage or economic loss resulting from destruction of valuable records including accounts receivable.

2. Cargo insurance is an inland marine policy covering the insured's products while being shipped or in the hands of a common carrier. Limits typically depend on the maximum value per shipment.

3. Leasehold interest insurance. This can be added to a commercial property coverage to protect when a favorable lease is terminated because of damage to the present premises and the firm is forced to pay a higher rent in the alternative premises.

Risk Management

4. Auto physical damage insurance. This is commonly added to the commercial auto policy to cover collision and comprehensive damage, losses, and vehicles, including the possibility of several vehicle losses in a single year.

5. Life and disability insurance on a key person, engineer, researcher, salesperson.

16.4(c): Available Coverages

Other insurance is available for losses which, though likely to be small or predictable, might have value to some businesses:

1. Credit insurance on loans to pay if that person dies or is disabled.

2. Glass insurance under commercial property coverages.

3. Depositors forgery coverage on incoming instruments.

4. Increased limits on medical or disability under auto and general liability coverages.

16.4(d): Summary

A typical business should allocate scarce premium dollars first to the essential coverages; second, to advisable coverage; and third, to the purchase of available coverages only under unique circumstances.

In the risk management decision process, the business will decide the best combination of insurance and other tools in each category.

1. Risks to avoid, prevent or control. For example, installation of automatic sprinklers, housekeeping, accounting controls, duplication, separate storage of valuable information, safety inspections, annual physicals, etc.

2. Risks to assume. For example, losses up to deductibles, losses in excess of limits of insurance purchased, losses excluded under insurance policies, and earthquake or flood losses.

3. Risk to transfer by contract with independent contractors, suppliers, customers, landlords, or tenants. Within the framework of the insurance and risk management program the business and consultant broker must purchase the insurance.

16.4(e)(1): Liability Management and Insurance

The answer to the question of "can you be sued?" is "yes!", and likely you and your firm will be named defendants. Whether you will be held liable depends on how well you managed the risks. Whether your liability insurance will respond to effectively defend you and pay claims depends on the quality of the insurance and services you purchased.

16.4(e)(2): Claims Prevention Procedures

The first line of defense for a business is to prevent the lawsuit. Often claims-prevention measures are remarkably simple and inexpensive when compared with the cost of litigation. "An ounce of prevention is worth a pound of cure." This involves removing or controlling hazards that make losses more likely to occur.

Many claims-prevention measurers are of general application, reducing the frequency of all categories of litigation. These include open communications and disclosure, clearly defined procedures, well-trained personnel and continuing professional development programs, scrupulous respect for personal and constitutional rights, audit of personnel and compliance procedures, product safety features, warning labels, and customer education to reduce the number of injury and product liability claims. Systematic documentation of decision-making, avoiding services to high-hazard clients/customers, and making appropriate referrals when requested services are beyond the firm's competence, also reduce the potential for lawsuits.

Early chapters outlined liability exposures businesses face from four common types of lawsuits: (a) discrimination, (b) wrongful discharge, (c) premises liability, and (d) products liability, and lists claims-prevention procedures tailored to preventing each of these types of claims.

16.4(f): Buying The Right Liability Insurance

Your insurance broker takes your insurance design tailored according to the above outline to a few insurers for premium quotes to determine a reasonably competitive cost. Selected insurance companies must be financially strong, provide good services complementing any consultant and broker services, and pay claims in a prompt, fair, and equitable manner.

Typically, the lowest premium is not the best buy, because the insurer does not offer solid financial strength, quality services, and reliable payment mechanisms. The business buyer wants a stable relationship with insurers, before, during and after liability claims. A risk management consultant or insurance broker will know the reputation of insurers and their history of relationship stability.

Business people should know coverage gaps (what they are not covered for) and what coverage is available for their particular needs. For each policy elected for purchase, a list of exclusions and a list of endorsements should be obtained. (Note that policy advertisements and coverage brochures buyers may see before receiving the policies, commonly show neither basic coverage exclusions nor available endorsements to expand coverage.)

Businesses can gain better liability protection by using the following procedures:

16.4(f)(1): Buy An Umbrella Liability Policy

Buy a personal and commercial umbrella liability policy with at least $5 million or more limits, and $50 million may be appropriate. An umbrella policy offers a blanket of protection for many personal and business activities, adding limits <u>excess</u> of underlying auto and general policy limits and providing <u>broader</u> coverage than underlying policies. For coverage beyond the scope of underlying policies, the umbrella drops down to a deductible commonly $1,000 to $25,000, to be paid by the insured. Umbrella coverage typically extends beyond the underlying general liability policy to, for example, an insured's activities as a small landlord for wrongful eviction or legal discrimination claims, and to suits alleging defamation, libel, or slander, and injury such as shock, mental anguish, mental injury, or humiliation. The umbrella also adds limits excess of underlying liability policy limits. Umbrella policies are available for businesses and individuals, and small business people should purchase a personal umbrella policy and a commercial umbrella policy. There are no standard umbrella policy forms.

16.4(f)(2): Important Legal Defense Services

The very important legal defense services are covered by underlying and umbrella liability policies, in addition to potentially catastrophic court awards. The defense services of the insurance company-appointed attorney are needed for any covered claim, even if the insured is not legally liable. Since the answer to the question of can you be sued is yes, even people with low net worth need the legal defense coverage which typically states, "The Company has the right and duty to defend at company expense any claim or suit for damages covered by this policy." The company will pay defense attorney fees, court costs, interest on judgments, reasonable expenses, some lost earnings, and bond premiums, commonly in addition to the primary policy and the umbrella liability policy limits. The policy also states, "We won't defend a suit or pay a claim after the limit of coverage has been used up paying judgments or settlements". Therefore, the umbrella preserves the defense services until the insurer has paid the policy higher limits. Having high policy limits helps avoid conflicts of interest between you and your insurer since any offers to settle are more likely to be within your policy limits, and jury awards are less likely to exceed your high policy limits.

16.4(f)(3): Post Claim Loss Reduction

Loss reduction involves post-claim activities planned prior to the claims. Subrogation in insurance provides loss payment from third parties. Arbitration, mediation, and public relations efforts are event reduction strategies. Catastrophe or contingency plans are a coordinated approach to liability loss reduction. A recent example is the Schwan's Ice Cream salmonella case and the excellent communication plans employed to keep the liability exposures managed.

After you are sued you must risk manage the defense even if the claim is covered by your liability insurance. You should consider further protecting your interests by hiring your own attorney to monitor the case in cooperation with the defense attorney hired by your insurance company. You should closely participate in your defense, and in writing, express to your insurer your interest in participating and being included in any claim settlement discussions. You will then be prepared for the Murphy Law, worst case scenario . . . your insurer refuses to settle, you are subjected to a trial and the verdict is far in excess of your policy limits, or damages are not covered by your policy, and/or your insurer failed to properly protect your interests. In other cases your professional/business interests might be better served by refusing to pay certain illegitimate claims particularly if your professional conduct is challenged. Your active participation in all of these post claim circumstances is a vital part of liability risk management.

16.4(f)(4): Employment Liability and Worker's Compensation Exclusivity

16.4(f)(4)(a): Employers Liability Coverage for Employees Injury

Employers' liability can arise from worker injuries and illnesses not covered by workers' compensation. Coverage for this "employer's liability" is reflected in the insurance policy title, "Workers' Compensation and Employers' Liability Insurance Policy". The employers' liability portion of the insurance policy extends some coverage when WCL is not the exclusive remedy.

16.4(f)(4)(b): Workers' Compensation Exclusivity May Bar Employment Liability

A workers' compensation claim alleging violence or sexual harassment in the workplace can provide a remedy for employees, and a shield form suit for employers. All state workers' compensation acts (WCA) make workers' compensation the exclusive remedy for employees' injuries as the quid pro quo for employers' paying benefits, regardless of the employer's or the employee's faults. The scope of employers' protection from trot suits through this exclusivity is unclear, as shown by the amount of suits involving the exclusive remedy defense. Arthur Larson devotes a 171-page chapter of his treatise to the exclusivity provision.[4]

Despite courts' and legislatures' broad interpretation of the exclusive remedy provision, a few exceptions have been recognized when the employer acts in a dual capacity toward the employee,[5] when the workers' compensation act is preempted by a federal act,[6] when the injury is essentially non-physical,[7] and when the employer commits an intentional tort.[8]

16.4(f)(4)(c): Job Violence –
Defense and Liability Coverage

An employee is assaulted in the company parking ramp; or a male supervisor bumps and touches a female subordinate and the employer does not intervene; or during a heated argument in the office, one employee pushes and injures another. Violence at work is increasing amid waves of stressful downsizing and restructuring. Violence resulted in 1,000 workplace fatalities and more than 22,000 cases of injury, in 1993, according to the U.S. Bureau of Labor Statistics. Employers are being held accountable for those incidents through state and federal occupational safety standards and expensive lawsuits. Experts in safety and security assist employers in this area of risk management. Employers develop safety policies, prepare for layoffs and train workers to protect themselves on and off the job. Self-defense training encourages assessing options and taking responsibility. Employers can provide safer premises, self-defense skills, and have insurance coverage for claims by injured employees. Training can make employees feel safer, more aware and self-confident. These and similar cases create potential liability, however, the state's WCA may be used to limit the employer's liability and prevent injured employees from recovering more than medical expenses and wage loss.

Employers in need of defense services may first look to the attorneys appointed by their workers' comp insurer to handle the claims, due to the exclusivity provision of the state's WCA. If the injury is the type covered by WCA, the employer's liabilities under

WCA are exclusive and district courts have no subject matter jurisdiction. In addition to cases involving bodily injury or death, in some states the WCA can also cover purely mental injuries of employees arising out of employment. This potentially covers a broad range of injuries.

However, the WCA does not cover injuries arising from personal animosity or domestic disputes that spill into the work place. For these types of suits, an employer needs a form of employment liability insurance to cover defense and any ultimate liability, and there may be no insurance coverage available. For example, intentional acts intending injury are typically excluded. These injuries are motivated by personal animosity or nothing identifiable, and have no work place genesis.

Employers should establish a record of work-related issues underlying potential injury and to support an argument that the injury was work-related and occurred for no definable personal reasons, in order to keep the cause of action within the confines of the WCA. Your defense counsel can plead WCA exclusivity as an affirmative defense to avoid a wavier or foreclosure of the employer's motion arguing WCA exclusivity. It is unclear whether exclusivity will extend to injuries sustained by sexual harassment victims. Many states that find sexual harassment compensable under their WCAs have denied tort actions because of the exclusive remedy provision.[9]

Some courts suggest that WCA precludes some common law claims and some disability discrimination claims, but not other state human rights claims. Further, WCA cannot preclude employment discrimination claims based on Federal statutes, since State worker's compensation statutes cannot displace or restrict the operation of Title 7 of the Civil Rights Act, the Americans With Disabilities Act, or other Federal anti-discrimination laws. Therefore, employers may be subject to claims under Federal law without protection of WCA exclusivity provisions and separate employment liability insurance is required.

16.4(f)(4)(d): Employers Liability Policy Does Not Cover Employment Liability

Although it is two coverages in one insurance policy title, "Workers' Compensation and Employers' Liability", it does not cover many employment-related liability claims. Under the "Employers Liability" section, coverage is extended only to non-workers' compensation claims resulting from job-connected "accident or disease, causing bodily injury or sickness" claims. Furthermore, it specifically excludes the following claims:

4. any obligation imposed by a workers compensation, occupational disease, unemployment compensation, or disability benefits law, or any similar law;

5. bodily injury intentionally caused or aggravated by you;

7. damages arising out of coercion, criticism, demotion, evaluation, reassignment, discipline, defamation, harassment, humiliation, discrimination against or termination of any employee, or any personnel practices, policies, acts or omissions . . .[10]

Employers must buy an Employment Practices Liability Insurance Policy to cover these types of claims.

16.4(f)(5): Liability Policy Coverages and Exclusions

Ask if coverage is available under the primary and umbrella policies for any of the loss exposures shown on the following sample list of typical exclusions, found in several liability policies:

1. Workers' Compensation (any residence employees?); Unemployment Compensation, Disability Benefits Law or similar laws; Liability to a Fellow Employee

2. Autos (owned, non-owned, hired, leased, used regularly)

3. No-Fault Medical or Income Loss

4. UM or UIM bodily injury from uninsured/underinsured motorists bodily injury

5. Motorcycles, Mopeds, Motor Homes, Recreational Vehicles, licensed for or designed for use on public roads

6. Aircraft; Larger Watercraft (owned, leased, rented, or regularly used); Recreational Vehicles (snowmobiles, ATVs, dune buggies, dirt bikes, etc.); Speed Contests or Races, Exhibits (except for sailboats); Unlicensed Motor Vehicles; Entrustment of Aircraft and Watercraft

7. Professional Errors and Omissions or Malpractice Liability

8. Directors and Officers Liability, except for religious, charitable, civic or non-profit organizations

9. Business Pursuits (any on-premises, such as sales, equipment repairs, etc.)

10. Business Premises: claims from incidents on your business premises

11. Employment suits: hiring, denying, terminating employees

12. Environmental Impairment Liability

13. Contractual Liability

14. Independent Contractors

15. Insured's Owned Property or Property in Insured's Care or Control

16. Home or Business Child Care Services

17. Business Liquor Liability

18. Pollution to Land or Water

19. Assessments of loss by associations of property owners

20. Child Molestation

21. Communicable Disease & harassment, including sexual and physical abuse

22. War or Nuclear Accident Liability

23. Punitive Damages

24. Intentional Acts, including sexual & physical abuse

25. Illegal Discrimination

Some coverage is typically available for exclusions 1. through 18.

16.4(f)(6): Illustrative Liability Endorsements

Elect coverage from a list of endorsements to tailor protection for your liability exposures. Most of these endorsements provide expanded liability coverage for an additional premium, but their availability varies by insurance company. As an illustration, a typical endorsement list to expand liability coverage under auto, homeowners, and other primary coverage includes:

a. Uninsured/Underinsured Motorist Protection
b. Farm and Ranch Endorsement
c. Personal Injury Liability
d. Additional Specified Locations Liability, owned or rented dwellings
e. Off-premises Structures
f. Contractors' Interest
g. Unit Owners' Rental to Other (Condominiums)
h. Joint Unit Owners
i. Additional Insured (Homeowners/Condominium Assn.)
j. Waterbed Liability
k. Rented Personal Property
l. Nurses' Professional Liability
m. Products and Completed Operations Exclusion
n. Act, Errors, and Omissions Exclusion
o. Home Day Care Liability
p. Workers' Compensation Coverage for residence/domestic employees
q. Limited Pollution Liability Coverage
r. Non-profit Board of Directors
s. Teachers', Athletic, Manual, or Physical Training Liability
t. Discrimination because of race, color, religion or national origin, except illegal discrimination.
u. Employment Liability

v. Environmental Impairment Liability

An RM consultant or insurance broker can review an exclusion list and an endorsement coverage list tailored for each policy you consider purchasing, to help select the best coverages.

This chapter does not address lists of endorsements and exclusions for property coverage, which can provide a similar guide to buyers of property insurance.

16.5: Administering Program

After establishing a risk management program, it must naturally be maintained, monitored, and adjusted. You will make improvements based on your own learning and experience. Also, insurance and loss prevention techniques must be modified as your business changes <u>and</u> as outside risks change. This is a continuing challenge, and a risk management consultant can often be very helpful in the process.

16.6: Premium Reduction Methods

16.6(a): General Methods

Premium reduction involves auditing insurance policies, analyzing claims experience, followed by drafting insurance and service specifications. Below is a representative list of techniques to reduce premiums and improve coverage:

a. Consolidate several insurance coverages into package policies and negotiate more favorable premium rates.

b. Set higher deductible on property and auto physical damage policies.

c. Terminate insurance on older vehicles.

d. Review and coordinate all policies, including the umbrella, general liability and professional liability policies.

e. Use a selective competitive bid process.

f. Install managed care and claims management programs on medical and disability health insurance, worker's compensation and general liability areas.

g. Pay premium over time.

h. Delete restrictive endorsements.

i. Audit insurance company audits.

j. Coordinate the services of advisors, brokers, consultants and insurance companies.

k. Apply risk control prevention and loss reduction methods.

l. Pay small worker's compensation claims directly to injured employees while processing all required notices, e.g. first report of injury and other reports to the state, to employees and to insurers.

m. Systematically audit claims and claims reserves established by insurers.

n. Obtain certificates of insurance from independent contractors and waiver of subrogation from lessors, and become a named insured on their policies.

o. Limit policy cancellation to renewal date, after a 60-day notice.

p. Require notification of certain offers or intention to settle liability claims 30 days prior to the insurer agreeing to a settlement.

16.6(b): Worker's Compensation Premium Reduction

Worker's compensation premiums can be reduced by working with your advisor/broker/consultant to apply the following techniques.

1. Negotiate to Reduce Premium Payments

   a. Obtain lower estimates of incurred losses of initial premium estimate by reviewing claim reserves.

   b. Use lower payroll estimates or favorable classifications for the insurer's initial premium calculation.

   c. Obtain depressed premium payment schedules and favorable dividend plans.

   d. Obtain decreases in other insurance.

   e. Accelerate retrospective premium adjustments if a return is due.

2. Audit Premium Calculations

   a. Audit premium base by:

      (1) dividing payroll among premium rating classifications,

(2) Excluding independent contractors' payroll,

(3) Obtaining certificates of insurance from independent contractors, and

(4) Maintaining evidence of other insurance.

b. Audit premium audits, billings, and retro adjustments. Annually obtain and review the experience rating form, which shows the three-year claims and payroll figures used to calculate your premium modification factor.

3. Monitor Claims

   a. Review reserves at least three months after policy expiration date, in time for an initial meeting and a follow-up meeting before unit loss reports are submitted, six months after expiration date. Incurred losses for the three years prior to the latest policy period are used to calculate the experience modification factor. These losses are undated 18, 30, and 42 months after policy inception.

   b. Review claim files for possible second injury recovery, subrogation, double payment, or double reserves from two insurers, noncompensability, statute of limitations (two years from injury date to make claim), reserves discounts, inaccurate or incomplete information. Don't ignore the small $1,000 to $5,000 claims.

4. Pay medical claims promptly and directly to employees, but make the regular first report of injury and other reports to the insurer and state Department of Labor and Industry.

5. Loss control methods to reduce cost include reviewing the following:

a. Second injury registration. Second injury fund provisions have been repealed in some states.

b. Brochure describing worker's compensation program.

c. First report of injury forms with:

   (1) witness names, photos, description
   (2) possible third party liability
   (3) assessment of rehabilitation prospects
   (4) second injury qualification possibility

d. Certificate of insurance form

e. Rejection of your worker's compensation coverage form for insured independent contractors

f. Definitions of an independent contractor and an employee

g. List of functional capabilities communicated to examining physicians

h. Letter and communications to injured employee and family

6. Prompt, effective claims handling.

   a. Immediate medical care

   b. Follow-up communication with employee and medical providers

   c. First Report of Injury Form, completed by trained persons and sent to insurer within 24 hours

7. Preselection of qualified rehabilitation consultants, independent medical examiners and legal counsel.

8. Return-to-work program.
   As soon as medically possible, in the most productive capacity possible, at work made available by the employer

   a. Adjust work hours or production quotas

   b. Modify work assignment to accommodate temporary work restrictions

   c. Explain to co-workers the reasons for special work assignments

   d. talk to a rehabilitation consultant concerning modifications of the former job

   e. monitor progress and keep supervisors informed

   f. coordinate your efforts with union work rules.

9. Loss prevention and loss control.

   Keys to preventing the injury, loss, claim, rehabilitation process

10. Individual case management.

    Team of specially trained medical practitioners, e.g. occupational nurse practitioner, to communicate with employees and medical providers and review cases each week for appropriate, fair and economical treatment.

Cost reduction and improved benefits are based on prompt, effective communication to employees and medical care providers.

16.7: Buying Risk Management Services

A business can retain an independent risk management consultant and/or insurance broker to identify problem areas and recommend appropriate risk management methods, including insurance. Independent consultants offer services on a fee basis, not a commission.

Small firms which cannot afford risk management consultant's fees may engage an insurance broker on a fee basis, with commissions on insurance offsetting the fees. The consultant/broker should have experience with your particular type of business. A consultant/broker can utilize the risk identification and premium-reduction methods outlined above.

Working together, businesses and their liability insurers can reduce the risk of lawsuits. Claims prevention measurers provide an inexpensive first line of defense. Careful selection of liability coverages and claims management provides the second line of defense, benefiting the business by increased coverage of claims and the insurer by increased insurance sales.

Risk management consultants/brokers who lead buyers through this process, permitting buyers to affirmatively elect and reject additional coverage, provide a valuable service and may reduce the possibility of errors and omissions claims against the agents.

1. The AMA Risk Analysis Guide provides a checklist of (1) possible assets and (2) possible exposures. This checklist, though very useful, is limited to property and liability exposures. The exposures to loss are categorized as (1) direct, (2) indirect or consequential, or (3) third-party liabilities with numerous subcategories.

2. A risk analysis questionnaire that contains a list of questions designed to (1) remind the corporate risk manager of possible loss exposures, (2) gather information that will describe in what way and to what extent the particular business is exposed to that potential loss, and (3) summarize the existing insurance program, including premiums paid and losses incurred (Pfaffle & Nicosia, 1977).

3. Minn. Stat. § 70.253 (1995).

4. 2A Arthur Larson, The Law of Workmen's Compensation Section 4.00 (1990) supra, note 100, sections 65.00-67.00.

5. See e.g., Douglas v. E. & J. Gallow Winery, 137 Cal. Rptr. 797 (Ct. App. 1977) (allowing an employee to successfully sue his employer when he was injured from a fall due to the collapse of an elevator scaffolding device that was manufactured by the employer, or nurse injured on the job in a hospital sues in the capacity of a patient treated by the hospital staff).

6. See, e.g., Adams Fruit Co. v. Barrett, 494 U.S. 638 (1990).

7. See, e.g., Livitsanos v. Superior Court, 828 P.2d 1195 (Cal. 1992).

8. See, e.g., Gulden v. Crown Zellerbach Corp., 890 F.2d 195 (9th Cir. 1989). (Holding under Oregon law that an employer who ordered employees to clean up a PCB spill without protective clothing may have intended that the employees be injured, and therefore denying the employer summary judgment); Cunningham v. Anchor Hocking Corp., 558 So.2d 93 (Fla. Dist. Ct. App. 1990). (Holding that suit alleging that employer diverted smoke stock so that fumes went into

workplace not barred); Kennedy v. Parrino, 555 So.2d 993 (La. Ct. App. 1989). (Holding that suit for intentional batteries by employer not barred or employee suits alleging false imprisonment for loss of freedom or defamation, for damage to reputation, or emotional distress caused by outrageous employer behavior.)

9. Lapinad v. Pacific Oldsmobile-GMC, Inc., 679 F.Supp. 991 (D. Haw. 1988); Ford v. Revlon, Inc., 734 P.2d 580 (Ariz. 1987); Hart v. National Mortgage & Land Co., 235 Cal. Rptr. 68, (Ct. App. 1987); Millison v. E.I. du Pont de Nemours & Co., 501 A.2d 505 (N.J. 1985); Hogan v. Forsyth Country Club Co., 340 S.E. 2d 116 (N.C. Ct. App. 1986); Palmer v. Bi-Mart Co., 758 P.2d 888 (Or. Ct. App. 1988).

10. Workers Compensation and Employers Liability Insurance Policy, p. 3 of 6.

APPENDIX 1

IMPORTANT NOTICE TO ALL PERSONNEL OF AJAX WRENCH COMPANY, INC.

Ajax strives to provide a good work environment for all personnel. If you, during the course of your work discover that you are the subject of any discrimination or unethical conduct, or matters that you consider a violation of the law, you should report such matter in writing to John Raymond, Senior Vice President, within thirty (30) working days of the discovery of such a violation.

If you observe any discrimination, sexual harassment, unsafe work conditions, tax law violations, or other illegal activities, you must report that condition. Reporting any such activity will not endanger your job or any of the benefits provided by Ajax.

The personnel of Ajax Wrench Company, Inc. will receive or have received a copy of this Notice and Agreement. A copy will be posted in each department, and if any of the personnel of Ajax do not receive a copy they should immediately request a copy from the personnel manager.

Please sign in the indicated space below and date and deliver to the personnel department. The personnel department will retain the original, but you will be given a copy at the time you deliver the original.

If you have any questions at all regarding this notice, you are to address those concerns in writing to: John Raymond, Senior Vice President in charge of personnel.

I HAVE READ THE ABOVE NOTICE AND UNDERSTAND IT, AND I HAVE RECEIVED A COPY.

Dated: _____   _____
                                                          Employee

APPENDIX 2

PART-TIME EMPLOYMENT AGREEMENT

Ms. Jane Goodhue
229 Liberty Street
Plainfield, New Jersey 07060

Dear Jane:

The following terms are understood to govern your employment for Mohawk Tool & Die, Inc.:

1. You are a part-time employee.

2. You will receive no benefits other than the hourly pay.

3. Hourly pay is $8.00 per hour.

4. Mohawk does not guarantee the number of hours or days that you will be employed.

5. You will be notified by the Personnel Department of your work schedule.

6. This part-time employment agreement can be terminated by either party with 24-hour notice in writing.

7. Mohawk strives to provide a good work environment. If you, during the course of your part-time employment,

Ms. Jane Goodhue
Part-Time Employment Agreement
Page -2-

discover you are the subject of any discrimination, sexual harassment, or any other conditions that you consider an ethical violation or a violation of the law, you should report such violation in writing to Sam George, Vice President of Personnel, within thirty (30) days after you discover such a condition.

Below is a place for your signature and the date that you received this notice. The original of this notice should be delivered to Sam George and it will be filed in the personnel records and you will receive a copy.

Very truly yours,

MOHAWK TOOL & DIE, INC.

By_____

Dated: _____   _____
                            Jane Goodhue, Employee

APPENDIX 3

SELECTION OF ACCOUNTING METHODS AS IT RELATES TO THE FINANCIAL STATEMENT
By: Mark Kallenbach, J.D., C.P.A.

Two businessmen, George Money and Gary Gish, are at lunch with their accountants kibitzing about the profitability of their businesses.

George says to Gary, "Gary, my company, Money, Inc. made $1,000,000 last year."

Gary replies, "George, that's great, but my company, Gish, Inc. made $2,000,000 last year."

To which George retorts, "Gary, we've been friends since childhood, and although I have known you to exaggerate a little from time to time, there is no way your company which does $5,000,000 a year in sales could ever be more profitable than my company which has sales in excess of $25,000,000. For you to believe that Gish's bottom line is greater than Money's is a wish."

Gary then explained to George that Gish's financial statements were prepared in accordance with something accountants refer to as generally accepted accounting principles, so his income as to be right.

Jon Peterson, Gish's chief financial officer explained that generally accepted accounting principles ("GAAP" - which is pronounced as "gap") are rules concerning how financial transactions are to be accounted for, as promulgated by the Accounting Principles Board ("APB"), its successor the Financial Accounting Standards Board ("FASB"), the American Institute of Certified Public Accountants ("AICPA"), and others who are interested in the rules concerning financial accounting. The APB, FASB, and the AICPA go to great lengths to research and articulate appropriate accounting rules and regulations to insure that all financial statements are accurately and uniformly presented using the same accounting principles or rules. The idea is that by having accountants apply GAAP, a uniform nationwide set of rules a reader or user of any given company's financial statements, will be able to accurately ascertain how a company is doing. GAAP requires that a business's profitability or loss, financial position, net worth, and use of cash and resources be disclosed.

Derrick Diligent, Money's chief financial officer responded to Jon's comment, adding that Money's financial statements were also prepared in accordance with GAAP. The difference was that Gish's income only appeared to be more than Money's. In truth and in fact, Money's income was more than Gish's in "real dollars" because Money elected to apply more conservative accounting principles than Gish. Money has adopted conservative accounting principles because:

(1) By applying the more conservative GAAP, the "quality" of Money's earnings was enhanced, "less is more" if you will;

(2) By applying conservative accounting principles and earning what appears to be less income, Money pays a smaller amount in income taxes than if more liberal accounting rules were applied;

(3) A further advantage associated with adopting conservative accounting principles is that Money does not have to keep two sets of books, one for financial statement purposes - those financial statements that are prepared for viewing by financial institutions or investors; and another set of "tax" financial statements which are prepared exclusively for tax purposes and based on the IRS Code.

Gary inquired of Derrick, "You mean to tell me that 'less can be more', and that it would be correct to keep 'two sets of books'?

Derrick replies, "Gary, that's right."

Gary reiterates to Derrick, "What you're talking about, this business of conservative versus liberal application of GAAP, coupled with keeping 'two sets of books' is very confusing, and in fact keeping a second set of records for the taxing authorities sounds illegal to me. Further, Sammy just said the purpose of GAAP accounting was to insure that if two different companies had identical operations, each company's financial statements would be the same! What you say makes no sense."

Derrick says, "Gary, let me explain. I'll use Money and Gish as an example of how the application of GAAP differs, but let me explain first how our systems are the same. Like Gish, Money utilizes accrual accounting. The purpose of accrual accounting is to match the revenues earned but not necessarily received in a given financial period against the costs or expenses associated with earning that income, even though those costs or expenses may not yet have been paid. For example, assume the period for the Statement of Income and Expense we are talking about ends on June 30, 1995. If on June 20, 1995 we shipped $100,000 of product, and received payment after June 30, 1995, we will still recognize $100,000 of income for the period ending June 30, 1995 because our customer has a legal obligation to pay us. Likewise, if Money receives an electric bill for $10,000 on July 5, 1995 for the month of June, Money will still show the $10,000 utility bill on its June 30, 1995 statement. Why? Because Money has incurred the obligation and used the utilities prior to June 30, 1995, therefore it is an expense for the period ending June 30, 1995. To recognize income when received or expenses when paid is what is known as being on the 'cash basis', and GAAP typically does not permit cash basis accounting because income and expenses are not allocated to the proper period in which the income was earned or the expenses incurred. As an aside, even though it fails to accurately depict income or expenses, from an accountant's perspective, the Internal Revenue Service has adopted something known as the 'modified cash basis', which is a cross between cash basis accounting and accrual accounting for determining income for taxation purposes. In any event, I think Jon would agree that both Money and Gish have correctly applied the concept of accrual accounting.

Jon says, "Derrick is right!"

Derrick says, "However, John and I part company in other areas concerning the application of GAAP. For example, Money values its inventory on the last in first out ("LIFO") basis, and Gish values its inventory on the first in first out ("FIFO") basis. The net result is that if both Money and Gish had identical physical inventories, for financial statement and taxation purposes, the valuation of the same identical inventory would be different, yet in accordance with GAAP and perfectly legal from a taxation perspective.

"Wait one minute!" exclaims Gary. You mean to tell me Money and Gish could have identical inventories, yet those inventories would be valued differently, and still be in conformity with GAAP? I don't understand!"

Jon: "Gary, Derrick is right. Let me show you why. Let's assume both Money and Gish have a beginning inventory of 1,000,000 units each which have a value of $2.00 per unit for a total beginning inventory of $2,000,000. Let's further assume each company purchases another 2,000,000 units for $3.00 each, and that each company sells 1,500,000 units for $5.00 each. Money is on LIFO, Gish is on FIFO."

Jon took George's dinner napkin, spread it out on the table and prepared the following comparative income statements on it:

	Money (LIFO)*		Gish (FIFO)**	
Sales:	1,500,000 units x $5.00 each	$7,500,000	1,500,000 units x $5.50 each	$7,500,000
Cost of goods sold:				
Beginning Inventory	1,000,000 units x $2.00 each	$2,000,000	1,000,000 units x $2.20 each	$2,000,000
Purchases	2,000,000 units x $3.00 each	$6,000,000	2,000,000 units x $3.00 each	$6,000,000
Goods Available for Sale	3,000,000 units	$8,000,000	3,000,000 units	$8,000,000
Less Ending Inventory:	1,000,000 units x $2.00 each		1,500,000 units x $3.00 each	
+	5,000,000 units x $3.00 each	$3,500,000		$4,500,000
Cost of Goods Sold:	1,500,000 units	$4,500,000	1,500,000 units	$3,500,000
Net Income:		$3,000,000		$4,000,000

* LIFO - Inventory that is oldest (purchased before any other inventory). Therefore, "last in" and is sold before newer inventory.
** FIFO - Inventory that is most recently purchased is sold before the older inventory.

Gary having had a chance to review Jon's Income Statement laments: "Wow, I can't believe it, in both cases the sales are identical, the units remaining in ending inventory are identical, the product received and shipped is identical, yet income is different by $1,000,000. Jon, are there any other things that GAAP accounting allows that will give identical companies with identical sales and expenses vastly different incomes?"

Jon: "Sure, Gary, depending on the nature of the given company's business, there are probably ten or more different ways the identical companies could treat accounting issues differently and still be in compliance with GAAP. Probably, the two most obvious and most frequent timing differences are in the area of inventory valuation and depreciation."

Gary: "Again, I don't understand what you mean. Based on your example about how FIFO and LIFO works, I think I can understand how inventories could be valued differently, but depreciation is depreciation. How can depreciation be calculated two different ways?"

Derrick: "Gary, let me take a shot at what Jon is trying to tell you. The FASB allows the accountant a fair amount of discretion in choosing how to apply GAAP to the company's financial transactions that he or she is analyzing and reporting. Generally speaking, regardless of how the transaction is recorded, in the end, it all 'comes out in the wash.' That's what Jon meant when he was talking about timing. Let's use depreciation for an example. Let's compare how Gish would depreciate, say a truck as compared to how Money would depreciate that same vehicle. Assume the truck costs $20,000, has a five-year life, and no salvage value. Money uses a conservative accounting method, let's say one hundred fifty percent declining balance[1], and let's say Gish uses straight line[2]. Here's how each company's depreciation schedule would look:

	Money		Gish	
	Depreciation	"Book Value" of Vehicle	Depreciation	"Book" Value of Vehicle
Year 1	$ 6,000	$14,000	$ 4,000	$16,000
Year 2	$ 4,200	$ 9,800	$ 4,000	$12,000
Year 3	$ 2,940	$ 6,860	$ 4,000	$ 8,000
Year 4	$ 3,430	$ 3,430	$ 4,000	$ 4,000
Year 5	$ 3,430	$ -0-	$ 4,000	$ -0-
TOTAL	$20,000		$20,000	

You will notice, in the early years, Money's depreciation expense is more than Gish's, but in the end it all works out. Both companies after five years write off the same $20,000. In the end the numbers all come out the same.

"In Addition to inventory valuation and depreciation, Gary and I could give you all kinds of other examples, but I think, gentlemen, that you 'get the drift."

---

[1] Declining balance: Total value on item to be depreciated with greater depreciation allocated to the beginning year and declining each successive year for the life assigned to the depreciated property.

[2] Straight line is equal depreciation each year for the life of the depreciated property.

George says, "Gary, I get it. I get it. I see how Jon does the numbers to make Gish's income more than Money's, but I don't care what anybody says. I still think Money made more money than Gish, Inc.; and furthermore, Money's net worth, by that I mean assets less liabilities is greater than Gish.

"George, be careful," interjects Derrick. "It is possible that because of the way Gish applies GAAP to its balance sheet, which is the financial statement where we accountants total up the business's assets against total liabilities to compute "net worth," that Gish's net worth is greater than Money's.

George says to Derrick, "No way, Money's plant is better and more sophisticated than Gish's. Money has more inventory than Gish. Money has more accounts receivable than Gish. Money has more money than Gish. Money has more of everything than Gish. The only thing Money has less of than Gish is liabilities and debt. Therefore, there is no way Gish's net worth can be greater than Money, Inc.'s. Lastly, remember the 40 acres we bought at 4000 Waterplace? That property is worth over $5,000,000, and we only paid $2,000,000 for it! That alone would give Money a net worth far greater than that of Gish, Inc."

Seeing that George was about to have a stroke, and yet wanting to be truthful with him, Derrick says to George, ""Cool down! Remember when we were talking about how it was possible for Gish to have greater earnings than Money? Remember how we concluded that Gish's earnings were just not the quality of Money's earnings? Well, the same thing can happen with the company's balance sheet!"

"Awe, c'mon, I don't believe it!" George says to Derrick.

"Yeah, it could be true!" Derrick retorts. "Here's why. Take another look at George's napkin which depicts how LIFO and FIFO work."

George: "So what?"

Derrick: "George, you see where it says 'ending inventory?"

George: "Yes."

Derrick: "Well, because Money on LIFO, ending inventory is $3,500,000. Because Gish is on FIFO, ending inventory is $4,500,000. Assuming everything else were equal, here's how Money's and Gish's Balance Sheets may appear:

	Money, Inc. Assets	Gish, Inc. Assets
Cash	$1,000,000	$1,000,000
Accounts Receivable	2,000,000	2,000,000
Inventory	3,500,000	4,500,000
Plant and equipment	2,500,000	2,500,000
Total Assets	$9,000,000	$10,000,000
	Liabilities and Stockholder's Equity	Liabilities and Stockholder's Equity
Accounts payable	$1,500,000	$1,500,000
Long-term debt	$2,000,000	$2,000,000
Total Liabilities	$3,500,000	$3,500,000
Stockholder's Equity	$5,500,000	$6,500,000
Total Liabilities and Stockholder's Equity	$9,000,000	$10,000,000

"As you see, based on the example I just prepared, Gish's net worth is more than Money's."

Gary: "Derrick, I see what you're saying, but in all fairness to George, I mean Money, what about the property Money stole at 4000

Waterplace? Money only paid $2,000,000. I know of companies that would kill you to own the property for $5,000,000.

Sammy: "Gary, let me explain. GAAP typically provides that an asset is carried on its financial statements at either it's historical cost - what the company paid for it - or the assets' market value, whichever is lower. Because Money only paid $2,000,000 for 4000 Water place, and because the market value of the property is greater than the $2,000,000 Money paid for it, GAAP provides Money has to carry the property on its books for $2,000,000."

George inquires of Sammy: "Yes, but that's not fair. The 4000 Waterplace is worth $5,000,000. By forcing Money to carry the property at $2,000,000, Money's 'actual' net worth is understated by $3,000,000. What you're doing is misleading the reader or user of the financial statements. The reader of Money's financial statements are led to believe Money's investment is 4000 Waterplace is only worth $2,000,000. If Money reports 4000 Waterplace according to GAAP, Money could be sued for filing fraudulent financial statements. Further, if Money wants to borrow against Waterplace, it looks crazy when a $5,000,000 asset is carried on the financial statements for $2,000,000!"

Derrick" "George, relax. Historical cost accounting is one of the pillars of GAAP. To deviate from GAAP in this area would lead the user of the financial statements and accounting system. Further, if you need to borrow against 4000 Waterplace, the lender is always free to get his own appraisal of the property. Lastly, even an accounting neophyte knows of the inadequacies of financial reporting based on historical cost.

George inquired of Sammy and Derrick: "If historical cost accounting is suspect, why doesn't GAAP change the rules?"

Sammy: "First, George, historical accounting is conservative accounting. Second, historical accounting prevents the accountant from manipulating income through arbitrarily valuing a company's assets. Lastly, historical cost accounting is older than you are. The bottom line is that historical cost accounting is here to stay even though everyone is familiar with its shortcomings."

George, "Gentlemen, this lunch has given me a stomach ache. Less is more, more is less. GAAP was designed to assure consistent financial statement presentation, even though it doesn't. To make matters worse, accountants tolerate and seem to encourage a system which does not fairly and accurately reflect the results of financial transactions. All of these arcane accounting rules are nothing more than a ploy for accountants to play with the figures and then rationalize what they are doing. I think GAAP is baloney! I know Money has more money than Gish. And I know Money's earnings are more than Gish's. And I know Money's net worth is more than Gish's. And I now know it is possible that Gish's financial statements may say otherwise, but I know what I know! By the way, I'm out of money, because I forgot my wallet at the office. Gary, can you buy lunch?"

Gary: "George, I'd love to but I don't have any money with me either."

Derrick: "I'd pay for lunch, but like Gary and George, I have no money or credit cards."

Jon retorts: "Gentlemen, all I have is five bucks. The bill is sixty, but wait, I have an idea. Say Waiter, we're regulars here and none of us have any money or credit cards, uh, is there some other way we can make book with you?"

Waiter: "Gentlemen, sure! Simply prepare your financial statements accurately and in accordance with GAAP. My credit manager and I will review them. If you net worth is 'healthy enough' and your income sufficient to merit credit, I can open a tab for you."

INDEX

Accomplice liability, 112
Accounting methods, 229-240. See also Audits
ADA. See Americans With Disabilities Act (ADA)
Advertising liability, 97-98
Age discrimination. See Discrimination
Age Discrimination Employment Act, 63, 72
Agreements. See Contracts/agreements
Alcoholism, as disability, 64
Americans With Disabilities Act (ADA), 64, 152, 212
Arson, 98, 109
Assumed name certificates, sole proprietorships, 2
Assumption of risk, 77, 89
Audits, 152
Automobile insurance, 115, 198-199
Bankruptcy, 102-107
    automatic stay, 103-104
    Chapter 7/Chapter 11, 102, 104-105, 105-106
    discharge, 105-106
    exempt claims, 105
    loan considerations, 106
    practical tips, 106
    subordination doctrine, 105
    voidable pre-bankruptcy transfers, 104
    voluntary/involuntary, 103
Bodily injury insurance, 97. See also Personal injury insurance
Breach of contract, 13, 20, 31, 172-173, 183-184

Bribery, 110, 111
Bulk Sales Act, 16
Business insurance, 95-101
    business interruption insurance, 200-201
    commercial property, 98-99, 200
    contractual liability, 200
    directors and officers liability, 100, 128, 132, 199
    employment practices liability, 66, 73, 101, 128
    general liability, 97-98
    professional liability, 199-200
    types of, 95, 101
    See also Health benefits; Unemployment compensation; Workers' compensation
Businesses, purchase or sale of, 16-17, 20
C corporations, 1, 4-5
    changing, 54
    taxes, 5, 7, 51-52
CERCLA. See Comprehensive Environmental Response Compensation and Liability Act (CERCLA)
CGL. See Commercial General Liability (CGL)
Chapter 7/11 bankruptcy. See Bankruptcy
Children
    injuries to, liability, 77-78
    as trespassers, 77
Civil Rights Act, 212
Claims-prevention tips
    contracts/agreements, 20-21
    discrimination, 66
    generally, v
    premises liability, 82-83

Index 243

    products liability, 92
    risk management, 204-205
    sexual harassment, 66
    wrongful discharge, 73
Clean Air Act, 111
Clean Water Act, 111
COBRA. See Consolidated Omnibus Budget Reconciliation Act (COBRA)
Commercial fire insurance, 98-99
Commercial General Liability (CGL), 97-98, 116, 128, 129-130, 199
Comprehensive Environmental Response Compensation and Liability Act (CERCLA), 80-81, 111
Confidentiality
    contracts/agreements, 15
    discharged employees, 72
Confirmations, in writing, vi, 20
Consolidated Omnibus Budget Reconciliation Act (COBRA), 124-126
Contractors. See Independent contractors
Contracts/agreements, 10-24
    buy and sell agreement, 201
    claims prevention, 20-21
    common types, 13-19
    confidentiality, 15
    confirmations, vi, 20
    consideration requirement, 12
    copyright, 48
    examples, 225-228
    franchises, 19
    general principles, 11-12
    for goods, 14

insurance, 18, 200
offer, 11
patents, 48
for services, 15
tort liability, 20
trademarks, 48
unenforceable, 12-13, 20
verbal/written, vi, 10, 11, 20
See also specific types of contracts/agreements; Breach of contract
Contracts for deed, 30-31
defaults, 31
grace periods, 31
Contributory negligence, 77, 89
Copyright, 42, 46-47
defined, 46
fair use, 46
insurance coverage, 47
practical tips, 48
registration, 47
works for hire, 47
written agreements/contracts, 48
See also Patents; Trademarks
Corporations, 3-4
boards of directors, 3, 4
defined, 3
foreign corporations, 4
shareholders, 3-4
See also C corporations; S corporations
D&O. See Director and officers (D&O) liability insurance

Damages, products liability, 89
Debts, liquidated vs. unliquidated, 40
Decision-making process, customer in, v-vi
Deeds, 27-28. See also Contracts for deed
Defense coverage, 129, 133, 207, 210-212
Destination contracts, 14
Directors and officers (D&O) liability insurance, 100, 128, 132, 137, 199
Disabilities discrimination. See Discrimination
Disability insurance, 115
Discharge, wrongful. See Wrongful discharge
Discrimination, 60-68
    age, 63
    claims prevention, 66
    by co-workers, 63
    disabilities, 64, 151-152
    disparate impact claims, 65
    employment exclusion, 66
    employment practices liability, 66
    gender, 62
    insurance coverage, 65-66, 72
    mixed motive cases, 65
    negligent supervision claims, 65
    notice of, example, 225-226
    permitted practices, 65
    protected groups, 61-64, 71
    racial, 61
    religious, 61-62
    by supervisors, 63
    written notification, 66

wrongful discharge, 72
See also Sexual harassment
Dividends, and taxes, 51-52
Doctrine of Comity, and group health insurance, 121
Documentation, v-vi
E&O. See Errors and omissions (E&O) liability insurance
Embezzlement, 109
Employee benefits
- administration, defined, 133
- exclusions, 133-134
- fiduciary liability insurance, 128, 199
- generally, 114-115, 128
- and risk management, 201
- typical policy, 132
- See also Health benefits; Retirement plans

Employee Retirement Income Security Act of 1974 (ERISA)
- application of, 56-57, 117-118, 155n2
- and employee discharge, 71
- exemptions, 160-162
- fiduciary duty, 167
- and fiduciary liability insurance, 134
- and health benefits, 116-117
- and state law, 185

Employer liability, 128-129, 209-213. See also Commercial General Liability (CGL)
Employment agreements/contracts
- at will status, 70
- claims prevention, 20-21
- estoppel, 70
- example, 227-228

generally, 17
wrongful discharge, 69-70
See also Independent contractors
Employment practices liability insurance, 66, 73, 101, 128, 130, 213
Enterprises, 111
Environmental crimes, 111. See also Pollution
ERISA. See Employee Retirement Income Security Act of 1974 (ERISA)
Errors and omissions (E&O) liability insurance, 137
Estoppel, employment contracts, 70
Excess and umbrella liability insurance, 128, 131, 135, 206-207
Extortion, 110, 111
Fair Labor Standards Act, 71
Family and Medical Leave Act, 71
Fire insurance, commercial, 98-99
Flammable Fabrics Act, 90
Forgery, 109
401(k) plans, 182
Franchises
    agreements/contracts, 19
    defined, 19
    entire business format, 19
    product distribution, 19
    types of, 19
Fraud, 108-109, 111
Garnishment, 38-40
General liability insurance. See Commercial general liability (CGL)
Goods, 14
Group health insurance. See Health maintenance organizations (HMOs)

Group life insurance. See Life insurance
Harassment. See Discrimination; Sexual harassment
Hazards, on business premises. See Premises liability
Health benefits, 99-100, 114-158
    administering organizations, 116
    COBRA, 124-126
    contractual provisions, 120-121
    coordination of benefits, 123-124, 139-152
    dependents, 122-123
    eligibility, 122, 156n10
    employee cost, 114
    employer liability, 128
    and ERISA, 116-118
    federal regulation, 119
    under general liability, 98
    and managed health care, 135-137
    practical tips, 152-154
    state regulation, 119-121, 142-144
    24 hour coverage, 139-151
    types of plans, 99-100, 115-117
    vs. workers' compensation, 139
Health maintenance organizations (HMOs)
    coordination of benefits, 123-124
    as health benefit, 100, 115
    legal obligations, 121-127
    as managed health care, 135, 136
    regulatory jurisdiction, 121
    state regulation, 119-120
    tort claims, 126-127
Hostile-environment claims. See Discrimination; Sexual harassment

Income taxes, 51-59
    tax evasion, 57
    violations, notice example, 225-226

Independent contractors
    agreements/contracts, 17, 20-21
    characteristics, 17

Injunctions, 44

Installment land contracts. See Contracts for deed

Insurance
    breach of contract, 20
    contracts, 18
    copyright, 47
    discrimination claims, 65-66, 72
    disparate impact claims, 65
    employee exclusion, 72
    employment exclusion, 66
    employment practices liability, 66, 73, 101
    generally, v
    intentional acts, 65, 72
    negligence, 65, 97
    personal injury, 73, 97-98
    premises liability, 82
    products liability, 91
    sistership exclusion, 91
    wrongful-discharge claims, 72-73
    See also Business insurance; Health benefits; Risk management; Title insurance

Intellectual property, 42

Internal Revenue Code
    Subchapter C, 4

Subchapter S, 4
See also C corporations; S corporations
Inventions. See Patents
Joint ventures, 1, 6-7
    components, 7
    defined, 6
    taxes, 55
    See also Partnerships
Labor Management Relations Act, 71
Leases, real estate, 31-32
    defaults, 32
    purchase options, 32
    quiet possession covenants, 32
    terms, 31-32
Liability. See specific types of liability
Life insurance, 100
Limited liability companies (LLCs), 1, 5-6
    duration, 6
    flexible LLC statutes, 56
    management, 5
    ownership determination, 5
    registration, 6
    taxes, 55-56
Limited partnerships, 1, 3
Loans, secured/guaranteed, 35-41
    bankruptcy considerations, 106
    business as debtor, 39
    collateral, 37-38
    default, 37-38
    employees as debtors, 39-40

garnishment, 38-40
personal guarantees, 36, 40
practical tips, 40
security interests, 37-38
simple loans, 35-36
Long-term land contracts. See Contracts for deed
Mail fraud, 108, 111
Managed care organizations (MCOs)
and HMOs, 135, 136
and liability, 135-138
and workers' compensation, 138
Medical insurance. See Health benefits
METs. See Multi-employer trusts (METs)
Mortgages, 26, 28-29, 33
Motor vehicle insurance. See Automobile insurance
Multi-employer trusts (METs), 162-165
National Association of Insurance Commissioners (NAIC), model bills, 120
National Traffic and Motor Vehicle Safety Act, 90
Negligence
contributory, 77, 89
discrimination, 65
insurance, 65, 97
premises liability, 77, 79, 82
products liability, 89
Noncompete agreements/contracts, 15-16, 20-21
Nuisances
attractive nuisance, 77
pollution as, 80
public vs. private, 80

Occupational Health & Safety Act (OSHA), 71, 81, 152
Partnerships, 1, 2-3
    defined, 2
    taxes, 54-55
    See also Joint ventures; Limited partnerships
Patents, 42-44
    applications, 43-44
    defined, 42
    infringement, 44
    inventorship proof, 44
    practical tips, 48
    written agreements/contracts, 48
    See also Copyright; Trademarks
Pension plans, 159-189
    administrators, 164
    breach of contract, 172-173, 183-184
    claims/litigation, 175-184
    as common law contracts, 170-172
    contracts/agreements, 173-175
    defective/misleading communications, 178
    failure to comply, 179
    fiduciaries, 165-70, 176-177
    fiduciary liability insurance, 134-135, 179-180
    401(k) plans, 182
    impermissible reductions, 179
    members, 165
    generally, 160-162
    multi-employer trusts (METs), 162-165
    prohibited transactions, 177
    social investing, 180-182

sponsors, 164
taxes, 56-57
trusts, 165
types of, 56
Personal injury insurance, 73, 97-98. <u>See also</u> Bodily injury
Personal property, vs. real property, 26
Pollution
chain of production, 111
as nuisance, 80
potentially responsible parties (PRPs), 80-81
premises liability, 79-81
successor liability, 81
as trespassing, 80
<u>See also</u> Environmental crimes
Preferred provider organizations (PPOs), 100
Premises liability, 75-85
assumption of risk, 77
children, injuries to, 77-78
claims prevention, 82-83
contributory negligence, 77
criminal acts, 78
customer injuries, 76-77
dangerous or defective conditions, 76-78
defense, 77
hazards, 76
insurance coverage, 82
negligence, 77, 79, 82
OSHA violations, 81
pollution, 79-81
tenant injuries, 77

trespasser injuries, 77-78
Premium reduction methods, 216-221
Products liability, 86-94
    assumption of risk, 89
    business-risk exclusion, 91
    claims prevention, 92
    consumer fault defense, 89
    contributory negligence, 89
    damages, 89
    design defects, 87
    failure to warn, 87
    insurance coverage, 91
    manufacturing flaws, 88, 90-91
    negligence, 89
    owned-products exclusion, 91
    parties liable, 88
    products-hazard exclusion, 91
    sistership exclusion, 91
    standard of care, 90
    statutory claims and defenses, 89-91
    types of claims, 86-88
    useful life statutes, 90-91
    warranties, 89-90
Property
    damage insurance, 97
    stolen, 110
    <u>See also</u> Intellectual property; Personal property; Real estate
Quit claim deeds, 28
Racketeer Influenced and Corrupt Organizations Act (RICO), 110-111
Racketeering, 110-111

Real estate, 25-34
- closings, 26, 27-28
- contracts, 18-19
- contracts for deed, 30-31
- foreclosures, 28-29, 33
- leases, 31-32
- mortgages, 26, 28-29, 33
- vs. personal property, 26
- practical tips, 33
- purchase agreements/contracts, 26-27
- purchases, 26-30
- title insurance, 30, 33

Retirement plans. See Pension plans

RICO. See Racketeer Influenced and Corrupt Organizations Act (RICO)

Risk management, 190-224
- administering, 216
- claims prevention, 204-205
- and communications, v-vi
- control methods, 195-197
- coverages/exclusions, 198-203, 213-215
- defense services, 207, 210-212
- endorsements, 215-216
- identification of risk, 191-194, 223 n2
- liability, 101, 197-216
- loss prevention, 195-196
- loss reduction, 197, 208
- measurement of risk, 194-195
- premium reduction, 216-221
- safety advice, 196-197

services, buying, 222
umbrella policy, 206-207
workers' compensation reporting, 197
S corporations, 1, 4-5
changing, 54
taxes, 5, 52-54
Self-help possession/repossession, 37-38, 40
Seniority, employee, 65
Service contracts, 15
Sex discrimination. See Discrimination
Sexual harassment, 60-68
claims prevention, 66
by co-workers, 63
employment practices liability, 66
notice of, example, 225-226
by supervisors, 63
and workers' compensation, 130-131
written notification, 66
See also Discrimination
Sherman Anti-Trust Act, 12
Shipment contracts, 14
Sick leave, 115
Social investing, 180-182
Social security benefits, 201
Sole proprietorships, 1, 2
defined, 2
requirements, 2
taxes, 55
Statutes
flexible LLC, 56

frauds, 11
standard of care, 90
useful life, 90-91
whistle blower, 72
Statutes of repose. See Useful life statutes
Successor liability, 16-17, 81, 88
TAMRA. See Technical and Miscellaneous Revenue Act (TAMRA)
Tax Equity and Fiscal Responsibility Act (TEFRA), 168
Tax identification numbers, sole proprietorships, 2
Taxes. See Income taxes; Internal Revenue Code
Technical and Miscellaneous Revenue Act (TAMRA), 125
TEFRA. See Tax Equity and Fiscal Responsibility Act (TEFRA)
Tenants, premises liability, 77
Title insurance, 30, 33
Tort liability, and contracts, 20
Trade secrets, 15, 16
Trademarks, 42, 44-46
    defined, 44
    fair use, 45
    infringement, 45
    practical tips, 48
    registration renewal, 46
    use in commerce, 45
    written agreements/contracts, 48
    See also Copyright; Patents
Training programs, 152
Trespassers
    children as, 77
    pollution as, 80
    premises liability, 77-78

UCC. See Uniform Commercial Code (UCC)
Umbrella liability insurance. See Excess and umbrella liability insurance
Unemployment compensation, 96-97, 201
Uniform Commercial Code (UCC), 14
Useful life statutes, products liability, 90-91
Verbal agreements/contracts, vi, 10, 11, 20
Violence at work, liability, 210-212
Warranties
    deeds, 27-28
    express, 90
    products liability, 89-90
Welfare funds fiduciary liability insurance, 134-135
Whistle blower statutes, 72
White-collar crime, 108-113
    accomplice liability, 112
    arson, 98, 109
    bribery, 110, 111
    criminal fraud, 108-109, 111
    criminal liability for business associates, 112
    defined, 108
    embezzlement, 109
    environmental crimes, 111
    extortion, 110, 111
    forgery, 109
    management liability, 112
    racketeering, 110-111
    receiving stolen property, 110
Wire fraud, 108-109, 111
Workers' Compensation

>benefits, 71, 95-96, 115, 139
>coordination of benefits, 127-135, 139-152
>employer liability, 96, 128
>and lawsuit recovery, 131
>and managed care, 138]
>premium reduction, 218-221
>and risk management, 197, 198, 209-210
>sexual harassment claims, 130-131
>state regulation, 142-144, 210-212
>tort claims, 126-127

Wrongful discharge, 69-74
>claims prevention, 73
>confidentiality, 72
>discrimination, 72
>employee exclusion, 72
>employment contracts/agreements, 69-70
>illegal purpose, 71-72
>insurance coverage, 72-73
>personal injury, 73
>statutory limitations, 71-72
>whistle blower statutes, 72